Natural
Approach

A Free-flowing Man's Guide To Courting Quality Women

iUniverse, Inc.
New York   Bloomington

Natural Approach

A Free-flowing Man's Guide To Courting Quality Women

iUniverse books may be ordered through booksellers or by contacting:

iUniverse
1663 Liberty Drive
Bloomington, IN 47403
www.iuniverse.com
1-800-Authors (1-800-288-4677)

Because of the dynamic nature of the Internet, any Web addresses or links contained in this book may have changed since publication and may no longer be valid. The views expressed in this work are solely those of the author and do not necessarily reflect the views of the publisher, and the publisher hereby disclaims any responsibility for them.

ISBN: 978-1-4401-1050-4 (pbk)
ISBN: 978-1-4401-1052-8 (cloth)
ISBN: 978-1-4401-1051-1 (ebk)

Printed in the United States of America

iUniverse rev. date: 11/11/2008

Library of Congress Cataloging-in-Publication Data has been applied for.

By

eNIGMA

Dedicated to:

This book is dedicated to men seeking fulfilling relationships with quality women and men wishing to maintain an existing relationship with quality women; to mothers who want their sons to have life-long relationships with quality women, and to sisters who wish the same for their brothers. Lastly, this book is dedicated to fathers who want to impart knowledge of women to their sons.

Contents

Instead of studying women, study what women respond to.

-eNigma

enig•ma – / Applies to behavior or utterance that is very difficult to interpret. /
/ Something that challenges ingenuity for its solution. /

in•ge•nu•i•ty – / A skill or cleverness in devising inventiveness. /

Foreword

Women are fascinated by an enigma. Somehow they feel it is their God-given right to know the unknown. By nature, they are curious and delight in obtaining firsthand information about things within and outside their surroundings.

Through my investigative research and personal experience, I have compiled a systematic approach, which if followed, will enable men to have fulfilling and lasting relationships with quality women. Most books about relationships or dating have information that teaches men how to maintain relationships, but won't show them how to build relationships from the ground up, or how to court quality women.

We now have those in relationships who have no idea how to sustain them, and others who wish to find that special someone, but are clueless about approaching and interacting with the woman of their dreams in the twenty-first century.

By the time you finish reading this book, you will realize the mistakes you've been making, and will be able to fine-tune your skills in order to avoid repeating those blunders. The principles within this book are scientifically and practically sound, and will enable you to correct the habits that have been costing you countless relationships. If you've never been in a relationship with a woman, you will learn what to look for and what to avoid in women. As you internalize my principles, you will slowly begin to view yourself differently and develop an elevated sense of awareness that will allow you to discern the fakes from the authentic, the phony from the genuine, and the deceitful from the honest. You will never let yourself settle for less than what you truly deserve, because you are about to decipher the behavioral patterns of the female gender.

- eNIGMA

Introduction

Attraction does not sustain a relationship. It is like a wildfire that eventually burns out. Desire is much stronger. It is like a warm, continuous flame that is self-sustaining.

- *e*Nigma

The Natural Approach guide is a nexus of principles that help men build fulfilling relationships with quality women. This method of courtship that I invented is called the eNigma Technique of Courtship or ETC. It is based on empirical evidence and uses a free-flowing approach to women. My principles have been tested on the frontlines of the dating scene, and are sound.

When you embark on studying human behavior, you have in essence begun your quest to become a behavioral scientist, whether or not you have any formal training. The ETC method in Natural Approach, enables you to make sound judgments regarding your relationships, and if my principles are correctly applied, you will see that they indeed are infallible and will yield the results you so desire.

There are some experts who teach men to emphasize on generating attraction within a woman; however, attraction alone from a woman does not sustain a relationship. In order for a woman to want to keep you, she has to find you desirable. Attraction is like a wildfire that eventually burns out. Desire is much stronger. It is like a warm, steady glow that is self-sustaining.

It is possible to be attracted to someone you do not find desirable. You see it everyday with drop dead gorgeous women on the arms of a man who could win an ugly contest. Why, you may ask, does this phenomenon happen? Because the women might be attracted to the men's accomplishments, status, humor, or influence in their community, but that doesn't mean they find these men desirable. Just at it is possible to be attracted to someone and not find the person desirable, it is also possible to love someone you don't like. Some women will even go as far as marrying men they aren't attracted to. These men might be good providers, but because sometimes women would rather have security in a relationship, they go against their natural instincts of courting a man they are truly attracted to. What ends up happening in most of these cases is that there often is someone else in the woman's life whom she finds desirable, and will find ways of expressing that to him. This happens even when a woman is in a committed relationship. The person she is committed to fulfills certain needs that the other person she desires cannot, and the reverse is true. Think about your previous break-ups and ask yourself why they ended on such a sour note. The reason is because you fell in love with someone, but didn't really get the chance to develop a liking for that person. It is easier to love someone than it is to like a person. There are even some parents who love their kids, but don't really like them. These parents love the kids enough to support and provide for them, and will even protect them from danger. However, they never make themselves accessible to these kids or spend quality time with them.

To like someone takes a little more work. Loving is easy because you can love someone from a distance. You all know some relatives that you love from a distance. You really don't miss them but you would reach out to them if they needed help and you were in a position to extend a helping hand. Liking someone means you are fond of that person. Just being around them gives you a sense of satisfaction and fulfillment. When you think of them, you don't even want to be interrupted by external factors. That's why it is important to be in a relationship with someone who desires you. When you desire someone, you not only like that person, but you also yearn to be with the same. It is a longing. It involves the force of physical appetite or emotional need. When a woman desires you, she is literally "sold-out" to you.

According to Robert Sternberg, a behavioral scientist, the romantic love that we desire is made up of three key elements which are: The emotional element, which involves self-disclosure and leads to connection, warmth, and trust. The motivational element, based on inner drives which translates to physiological arousal. The cognitive element, which is the decision to love and stay in love with the beloved. It translates to commitment. So every time a relationship of yours didn't work out it's because, while your mates may have been attracted to you, they weren't sold out to you. The cognitive and emotional elements were missing. This is the problem that most men in the dating community are having. They are able to attract a quality woman using superficial means or their dynamic personality, but are unable to hold on to her. Even the so-called experts can't seem to sustain long-term relationships, because the attraction phase is about as far as they can go. The good news is that I am here to make a difference in the choices you've been making and the way you approach women and relationships in general. You will learn how to approach women in a free-flowing natural way. Your appeal will emanate from within. The advantage of the natural approach is that when a clinically sane woman is sold out to you, you can never lose her to someone else, unless you choose to. She will be loyal to you even if you've lost your job, if you are in poor health, or even when you do something to embarrass yourself. Women are instinctively attracted to certain qualities that manly men exhibit. If you can accentuate these traits, you will increase your chances of landing your ideal woman and her wanting to keep you.

In December 2004, I was in Wimbledon, England, and went to a pub. I had a conversation with two gentlemen. One of the guys told me a story about how he met his ex-girlfriend. He worked for a prestigious company and was earning a comfortable living. He used his status to attract her. She even talked about marrying and having kids with him. Something then happened as they were dating. They went to a soccer match and she happened to meet one of the footballers. Somehow she was able to contact him and amazingly the two started courting. The gentleman telling me this story continued to say that he was devastated by the breakup, but what shocked him the most was when he happened to run into her in Central London, she took a look at him then looked away like she had never seen him before.

He had used status and accomplishments to attain her, and that was the very tool someone else with higher status used to displace him. I want to de-program you from your old way of thinking, and re-program you to be selective in the kind of women you date. I will show you what to look for and what to avoid in women. You should also know when to end a relationship that is draining you emotionally. I don't want you to be the kind person who gets so jaded by relationships, because you failed to walk away from an unhealthy relationship

Chapter 1

Natural Approach

The truth that every woman responds to is purity of intention, and the essence of what you embody as a man of substance.

- *e*Nigma

It is not important to end up with a good woman, it is more important that you end up with the right woman. A good woman may not necessarily be the right one for you, however, the right woman will energize you. She will challenge you to conquer your horizons, and also inspire you to love. You will cease to experience mere existence, and actually begin to live life and celebrate its simple pleasures.

Before you make your approach, you have to determine the qualities you want in a woman, and the ones you do not want. A lot of people get involved in relationships that eventually fall apart because, even though they knew what they wanted in a woman, they failed to identify the qualities they did not want in her. Eventually when it's too late and they are in too deep, they realize that the person they are with has vices that outweigh their virtues. They either end up settling for less, or getting burned and becoming hostile toward women. It is also very important for you take an inventory of yourself and purge any traits, habits, or behavior that you find repugnant. This step is crucial if you expect to have a fulfilling relationship, because if you ignore it, the law of attraction will become effective which simply says, "You attract who you are." If you are flaky, how can you expect to attract someone who keeps her word? If you have a bad attitude, why should you expect to find someone who is kind, compassionate and understanding? If you aren't loyal, why do you feel entitled to someone with loyalty? You cannot feel entitled to such a person if you yourself haven't taken steps to improve your inner man.

Once you've done the necessary work and are proud of who you are on the inside, the outward factors will take care of themselves. Your outlook on life will be positive yet realistic. People will begin to notice a certain sincerity in your eyes without you saying a word. Your words will have depth, and not only will the listeners be able to hear them, they will also feel those words resonate within their souls. Your behavior will become natural and relaxed because you have now become whole. You'll automatically start to invest time in your physical appearance and clothing, your health, your eating habits, and will have a hunger to expand your knowledge base. It is the natural aura you exude, that will cause women to respond to you. I've noticed that in order to impress each other, some people would rather be accepted for who they are not, rather than be rejected for who they truly are. Most women have had to deal with men who are phony and have no substance, so they instantly can detect truth, when it's in their presence. The truth that every woman responds to is purity of intention, and the essence of what you embody as a man of substance. Reading this book is a step in the right direction.

When any woman first lays her eyes on you, married or single, she immediately determines whether or not you are someone with whom she can be intimate. This usually happens within the first five seconds. It all depends on how she perceives you. If you display a calm self-assured persona that is unpretentious, she will find you desirable. Now just because a woman finds you desirable doesn't mean she will follow through and act out her fantasies. The majority of women delight in keeping their fantasies to themselves because the fantasies tend to be extreme. Some women who are already spoken for might use those fantasies as a catalyst to ignite the passion they once had, if it was lost from the relationship they are currently involved in. I am personally against pursuing women who are already in committed or long-term relationships. It's best to court a woman who is emotionally available.

Once you have spotted a potential mate, let her give you the green light to make the approach. This is very important because when a woman likes you, she will make it very easy for you, and become readily accessible to you. I know you're thinking that you've been taught to approach a woman within the first few seconds even without establishing proper eye contact. Let me ask you a question. How many times did you approach a woman like that, and got her phone number, but when you called you got her voicemail? Or let's assume you were able to get her on the phone and even set up a date. How many times did a woman call you thirty minutes before the date and come up with an excuse as to why she couldn't make it? Getting a phone number from a woman is no big accomplishment. As a matter of fact, the majority of women will give you their number, just to be polite. Even married women will at least give you a work number. So rather than be presumptuous and approach her immediately to give the impression of confidence, let her invite you in her world. You may be wondering how that works. Well, when a woman finds you desirable and you are in close proximity with her, she will gaze at you intermittently, even if she's with another guy. If a woman is not interested in you, she won't even acknowledge your existence. Everything you'll ever need to know about a woman lies in her eyes and tone of her voice.

I remember some years ago, I worked for a certain entity and the top female supervisor was extremely rude to everyone. Nothing we did was ever right in her eyes, so I thought. She was your typical alpha female…all things alpha. Nevertheless, I remained diligent in all my work, even though I was a brand new hire. There was one thing however, she couldn't hide. She tried as hard as she possibly could, but I could tell she wasn't doing a good job hiding it. It was the look in her eyes when she spoke to me. The tone in her voice said one thing, but the look in her eyes betrayed her. Her eyes were filled with fire and raw passion. Her unjustifiable rudeness toward me was her way of masquerading the strong desire she felt for me. I could tell there was a battle going on within her.

As time went by, all that resistance crumbled and she went from being rude to being pleasant toward me. Even though I was her subordinate, she eventually started acting in a submissive and playful manner around me. The deep respect she had for me was as a result of her noticing that I was unfazed by her attitude. When I stated an opinion or suggestion, I was respectful but assertive. I was the only person who wasn't trying to seek her validation or approval. An alpha female will always be drawn to an alpha male, no matter what her orientation is.

After you have established the eye contact, you have to maintain it with her. The mere act of doing that will trigger curiosity as to whether you are looking at her because you know her from somewhere, or if you are simply interested in her. The fact that she maintained eye contact with you is the only green light you need to make the initial approach. How about if it's during the night at a social event and the lighting isn't good enough to allow you to establish clear eye contact? In such a scenario, you have to position yourself strategically at an angle where she will turn her head toward you. Because humans have peripheral vision they tend to shift their gazes along with their heads involuntarily. The only time the eyes shift without the head, is if someone is cheating on a test and doesn't want to get caught, or if you cut off someone in traffic and you both end up at the same traffic light, and their car is beside yours. Back to the night scene. Eventually, this girl at the social event will shift her head toward you. When that happens, don't approach her yet. There is a method to my madness. The reason you shouldn't approach her immediately is because you do not want to give her the impression that your world revolves around her. She might misread that as neediness. She's the one who looked your way, so she invaded your space. That means the ball is now in your court. You are now the one who decides when to approach, and you will do it at your own choosing. Remember, this is a situation happening at night, under bad lighting. If the lighting is clear, stick to how you would approach her during the day.

At this point in your life, you will have acquired the necessary tools to ignite a stimulating conversation, because you worked on your inner self and also expanded your knowledge base, as I recommended at the beginning of this chapter. It is the new and improved you. Now, walk confidently to her, and talk about any random observation you have made in the vicinity. If she's in a group, ignore the entire group; they'll get the point. Just focus on her and talk about anything but yourself. The reason is because you want to confirm that the green lights she gave were genuine. If she's interested in you, she'll begin to ask you personal questions because you've been audacious enough to interact with her even though she is a total stranger. Hold a conversation with neutral topics because you have to give yourself the chance to study the tone in her voice as she responds, and also the look in her eyes. If the two of you are seated, that is very good, and if you are walking, slow the pace down. If she's not wearing a ring on her finger, you have to assume that she is available unless she mentions she has a boyfriend. It is important to develop the art of being a conversationalist, because it will come in handy during this initial interaction. It can happen anywhere even on jogging trail when you 're sweaty and unprepared for such an encounter. If I told you the exact words to use, your approach would cease to be natural and free-flowing, and would come across as contrived. I cannot predict the kind of place you will meet the woman of your dreams. The important thing is to start a conversation about something you have observed that pertains to the particular vicinity you meet her, and maintain eye contact. This will later on serve you well because in the subsequent conversations, she will associate that vicinity with you. It's up to you to be creative enough to cause that initial approach to be engrained on her mind. I am sure you can recall exactly where you were when you first kissed a girl, or if you are married, you clearly remember where and how the proposal happened. That's the kind of emotion you want to evoke in her when she associates the vicinity with you.

If you're standing in line in a bank, you might mention that if they increased the number of tellers, it would help expedite the process. If you're in a grocery store, talk about an item you have purchased or intend to purchase. Let's say you're in a classroom, don't talk about your major, focus on her interests and be sure to ask her why she chose that particular major. Perhaps she's someone you work with. Since you already have rapport with her, state a positive observation you've made about the company and engage her. The words will flow through you naturally. This is just an icebreaker. One thing you have to understand is that women prefer to be in relationships with men who have a deep understanding of women. A woman's strength comes from her hope, that's why when faced with doubts, women have the need to be reassured. There are times in a relationship when a woman will tell you that she doesn't think you really care about her, or if you ask her what's wrong she'll say nothing's wrong. When women make such statements, they do it out of frustration and simply want your affirmation. This can be done by simply listening without offering advice, or having empathy toward her in whatever it is she is going through. When you make your selection of the kind of woman you want, you'll be a lot happier with someone who isn't regimented. Someone who is adaptable and comfortable in her own skin. But you also want someone who doesn't take herself too seriously to the point where you have to walk on eggshells in everything you do or say. By nature women are playful. They like to giggle. Every now and then they want their inner child to come out and play. It's the reason why even a grown woman will delight in sitting on your lap, if she's fond of you. That is something that little girls do with their parents or relatives. However, no matter how old a woman gets, she never outgrows her inner child.

Not all women are sweet and tender. There are those who are just outright mean to other people. The easiest way to detect this trait is to take a woman you are interested in to a restaurant on a date and observe the way she treats the wait staff. Some can conceal their meanness initially, but it will eventually show itself usually within the first three weeks. Others have a cold look in their eyes. I wouldn't recommend getting in relationships with these kinds of women, and that should be a red flag that such a person is hurting on the inside. Hurting people will either say hurtful things to you or about you, and to a certain extent they might eventually hurt you. Because you are whole, you deserve to be with a quality woman who is whole like you. If a woman doesn't take the necessary time and effort to work on her inner self as you did to become whole, you shouldn't waste your time trying to fix her. Find someone who is emotionally sound, and clinically sane. Don't be blinded by her looks or status.

On October 15, 2005, I was traveling by train from Venice, Italy to Rome. I boarded the train at Santa Lucia in Venice, but we also had to make a stop at Santa Maria Novella in Florence. Because I had done a lot of walking during the day, I was exhausted and decided to nap on the train back to Rome. A certain young couple boarded the train when we arrived in Florence, and sat directly opposite me. As we continued to wait for the passengers to get on board, there was a lot of chaos at the Santa Maria Novella train station. It was being caused by soccer fans at the station, because the soccer team from Rome had just won a match. There were several of these fans boarding the same train I was on, and they too were headed to Rome. I was the only black guy on the train, so anything was bound to happen with these drunk and rowdy soccer fans. There are a lot of pickpockets in Italy who are mostly gypsies. They beg for money in public places, and if you are not careful, they will pick your pockets too.

So I was on this train on my way to Rome, and it was already dark outside. My bag was between my feet, and the shoulder strap was wrapped around my right thigh, that way nobody could steal it in case I fell into a deep sleep. Just as was dosing off, and close to falling asleep, the couple sitting opposite me tapped my boot, and I ended up waking up. I stayed awake for about twenty minutes, and as I was slowly dosing off with my head tilted to the right, I once again felt a tap on my feet, and I awakened. I thought perhaps this couple was accidentally tapping my feet as they were shifting their legs. All along the soccer fans were basking in their victory chanting, "Roma! Roma! Roma!" I was oblivious to all that was going on around me because I just wanted to get some sleep. People were walking in the aisles from one cabin to another in the spirit of celebration. It takes two hours to get from Florence to Rome using the EuroStar train, so for all those two hours, I felt that tap on my feet until we got to Termini train station in Rome. Those continuous taps prevented me from fully falling asleep even though I desperately was hoping to get some sleep.

When the train came to a full stop, the couple that was tapping my feet stood up and smiled at me, and without saying a word, they left and disappeared in the crowd. It was minutes later that I was suddenly hit with a revelation. Those taps were not accidental as I had previously thought. They were intentional. This couple was simply looking out for me, because they knew that if I had fallen asleep, I would have been vulnerable to the pickpockets on the train. A common tactic that pickpockets use is to pretend to bump into someone and snatch the victim's wallet or purse. They may also cut a hole in one's luggage, and feel around with their hands for anything valuable. Needless to say, I was never able to say thank-you to the couple for their kindness in disguise, because their pure intentions only dawned on me long after I had left the train station and was in my hotel room.

The right woman for you will have your best interests at heart and will look out for you. Her motives will be pure and you won't have to second-guess her. Your triumphs will become her triumphs and she will also share your sorrows. A good woman might celebrate your victories with you, but when you experience loss, especially if it is job-related, she won't want to stick around because she doesn't want any part of you sorrows. I'm sure you've met someone who responded to you positively in the good times, but when times got rough and you were running a tight ship, she pulled a disappearing act. How did that make you feel? This just doesn't happen in romantic relationships, it happens also in all other facets of life. Perhaps it was a job and you thought because you had been loyal to your boss and had accumulated several years under your belt with their firm, he or she would return the loyalty. However, when you needed the job the most, you were downsized, and to make things worse, a surrogate was used to break the news to you. You didn't get a watch or even a company pen for your services. That's the same feeling you have when people give you the impression that they have your best interests at heart and it turns out to be untrue.

People will tend to take you more seriously if the quality of your life is better than theirs, or if you have a network of influential people in your life. King Solomon comments on this phenomenon when he says, "Everyone tries to gain favor of important people; everyone claims the friendship of those who give out favors." If you are perceived to be important, people will go out of their way to extend their friendship to you. What if you are not important and are an ordinary guy like the rest of us? That's even better because it allows us to filter the fake people from our lives. Eventually when you build relationships, they will be very fulfilling and long lasting because you know that the people in your life are there out of pure intentions, not because of your status in society. Your goal is not to just be friendly in your approach, but to extend your friendliness to as many people as possible, without any expectations or pre-conditions. Don't do it out of expectation of reward because you will set yourself up for disappointment. There are some people you will meet who are naturally ungrateful and are hard to please, and the more you give to them, the more they'll expect you to give. These kinds of people have a sense of entitlement. Nevertheless, be friendly toward them, even though you don't have to be their friend.

When you are friendly, you automatically become approachable. You don't have to walk around smiling to appear friendly, it is something you internalize, and it manifests itself in your physical countenance, especially when you are whole and well balanced. If you are a person who holds grudges, manipulates others, or abuses your position of authority, no matter how successful you become, you will never have the countenance of someone who is whole. When you smile, your smile will appear superficial and shallow because it fades away quickly. A true smile emanates from within. When someone has a genuine smile, even his or her eyes smile. You can actually hear a smile when you are talking on the telephone with someone who is authentic. Emotions have a very strong presence, the same way thoughts do.

During your initial approach, as you keep the conversation going, avoid touching her because your goal is not to create an external physical bond with her, but to create an internal bond that will manifest itself physically. You see women enjoy being romanced mentally that's why you never want to rush things when you meet a quality woman. When you start getting physical with her during your first encounter, she subliminally gets the interpretation that you are more interested in the physical aspect of her. She may not visibly react, but I can guarantee that when you call her, she won't answer her phone, or she will cancel a date with you. Women do not like to be objectified. They want to be appreciated for their true worth. As man of quality, you have to separate yourself from all the other men who have previously approached her. The way to do that is to focus on the intangible. It is possible to meet a woman and even kiss her during the first encounter; you might even be able to convince her to have a one-night stand with you, but after that encounter, you will never hear from her again. Some men get confused as to why they aren't hearing from the woman who was very receptive to them during the first encounter, and fail to realize that the woman was simply caught up in the moment. Once a woman has had time to think things through, it will be very difficult for you to win her over, because you were more interested in the external, and failed to connect with her inner realm.

As you continue to interact with her, avoid complimenting her physical attributes during this first conversation. If you do, you'll appear to be someone seeking her approval, which will translate into neediness in her mind. Spare the compliments for next meeting and be sure to only compliment her intangible attributes. These include humor, intellect, creativity, personality…you get the drift. A quality woman who is just as beautiful on the inside as she is on the outside, already knows that she's beautiful, so you don't have to remind her of that. All the other men she interacted with before she met you have complimented her about her physical beauty. What you have to do is to overlook that obvious quality and tell her something about herself she may not already know. Your goal during this first interaction is to get her contact information in order to set up a real date. Earlier on I mentioned that you should avoid talking about yourself, this is because if she's eager to want to know more about you, she'll be eager to make herself accessible to you for the next meeting.

There are several ways of getting a woman's phone number, you can improvise and find out which method is more effective. Some people use the direct approach, for example you might say, "I've enjoyed talking to you and would like to meet you again, what's your phone number?" Or what I find to be the most effective way of getting a woman's phone number, right before I conclude the conversation in the initial approach, I'll pull out my cell phone and hand it to her and say, "Go ahead and enter your phone number in there, so we can keep in touch." I've used this in college classrooms, at parties, at the airport, in department stores and it always works. In order for you to get results, you have to use those exact words. They portray confidence. You are actually inducing her to give the number to you on her own volition by handing her your phone and saying, "Go ahead and enter your phone number in there." The second half of the statement says, "So we can keep in touch." Right there, you have given her a justifiable reason as to why she should give you her phone number.

As a behavioral scientist, I've noticed that people tend to seek justification for their actions. I see this happening all the time in the marketplace. For instance, you might go into a store looking for a piece of equipment or electronic device, and find two that are similar, but one is more expensive than the other. It could even be a car at a dealership that you are looking at. The very first thought that goes through the human mind is, "How kind I justify spending this kind of money?" Even Bill Gates, one of the world's richest men, if he happened to do his laundry and forgot a twenty dollar bill in his pocket, then removed his clothes from the washer to put them in the dryer and discovered the wet twenty dollar bill, do you think he would just throw it away because his rich? Certainly not! He'd stretch it out, then place it in the sun until it dried, and put it back into his wallet, because he can't justify throwing away the twenty dollar bill simply because it is wet and wrinkled, and he's rich. As I write this book, I am personally going through a situation where I am trying to justify something. I have a very good digital camera that is 7.2 Mega Pixels, and there is another one of the same brand that is 10.4 Mega Pixels. Even though I can afford it, I have no justifiable reason to purchase it yet because the camera I have does an excellent job.

There is a third way of getting a phone number. Let's say you're about to conclude your conversation and already have a pen handy, you can reach for your wallet and pull out a piece of paper, even if it is a receipt, you then hand her the pen and paper and use the same statement as the one when handing her the phone. You will almost always have a 100 percent success rate in getting phone numbers if you follow my principles. There are exceptions though. If she's married, she'll tell you right away, and if she's in a committed relationship, she'll most likely just give you her e-mail address.

Anytime a woman gives you her e-mail address instead of her phone number it's because she already has a boyfriend, or she just got out of a serious relationship and hasn't yet received closure. Once you get her phone number, don't bother asking for the e-mail address because you don't want your relationship to be regulated by the electronic media, it is best to meet and talk with her in person. You also eliminate the possibility of her using e-mail as a means to flake on you or dilute the communication process. I also advise against text messaging because it removes the element of mystery and makes you readily available which is something you want to avoid during that honeymoon period of about 90 days. When you have solidified your relationship with her and she's your girlfriend, you can then add e-mail and text messaging as a mode of communicating to each other. They have to be used sparingly though, based on your good judgment.

After she gives you her phone number, I would recommend that you place a call right away, in her presence, so that your number will be logged into her phone. If the number she gives you is legitimate, either her phone will ring in your presence, and all she has to do is enter your name in her address book, or if she has a land line, your name and number will be logged into her Caller ID.

By this time you should already know each other's names. You should have asked her name during the first few minutes of the conversation. The purpose of asking for her name is to use it as a reference point in arranging your phonebook. Your phonebook at some point is going to have duplicate names of different girls. To solve that problem, if you meet a girl named Celeste at the bank, the phone entry would be: Celeste Bank. If you meet another Celeste at the movies, the entry would be: Celeste Movies. If you meet one at work, the entry would be: Celeste Work, and so on. Don't worry whether she asks you your name or not. Once you have the relevant information to contact her and you do so, she will be able to associate the place you both met with you. If she asks you your name during the conversation, that's a very good sign that she'll make it easy for you to access her. The initial approach should last anywhere from five to eight minutes, then you can arrange meeting her at a place that is conducive for a more lengthy conversation.

There are men who have asked me if it's recommended to either keep the phone number of an ex-girlfriend in one's phonebook, or if one should delete it. The answer is yes and no. If you were the one who broke up with her, keep the phone number that way if she calls, you'll have the discretion to answer the phone or not. If she's the one who broke up with you, delete the phone number, that way you'll receive closure faster, because you'll have no means to contact her. Never memorize a woman's number because if things don't work out, it will take you almost two years to erase it from your mind. Only memorize your relative's numbers and the women you aren't attracted to.

Chapter 2

What Women Respond to

Two of the most important things for a woman in a relationship are the need to feel secure, and the need to feel relevant.

- *e*Nigma

On Christmas day in 2005, I was with my family, and traditionally those who are skilled at cooking, bring something to eat. That day my mother cooked rice for us. One of my favorites foods is rice, and I just couldn't get enough of my mother's rice. At the end of the day I asked her what ingredients she had used to make the rice so tasty. She told me the exact ingredients and even showed them to me in her pantry. Initially I had planned to take them with me, but because I was flying back to Houston, I didn't want the airport security to mistake those herbs and spices for something else. I decided to write down the ingredients and the entire procedure she used to prepare the rice.

When I arrived back in Houston, I was determined to duplicate the meal my mother had prepared that Christmas. I went to the grocery store and purchased everything I needed as my mother had instructed me, then I even called her and mixed the ingredients while she was on the phone. After I hang up, I let the rice boil along with everything else I had added.   When the meal was ready, I served it and to my disappointment, it was nothing like what my mother had prepared. I couldn't understand how I failed to duplicate her meal even though I did exactly was she told me, and even had her on the phone instructing me.

A few days later, I invited some friends to my place for lunch. I had already decided in my mind that rice wasn't one of the dishes I was good at preparing, so I focused my efforts on cooking other meals I was good at. For the sake of variety I also cooked a little rice using the same recipe my mother had given.

On the day of the invitation, my friends arrived and served themselves a little bit of everything I had cooked, including the rice. At the end of the day, I was surprised about what my friends commented regarding my cooking. They all unanimously said that of all the meals I had prepared, they enjoyed my rice the most. I was shocked. I couldn't believe what I was hearing. I had been disappointed in myself because I thought I had failed miserably to duplicate my mother's cooking.

You see I got it right the first time but didn't realize it. As I was cooking, the aroma of the rice satisfied my hunger mentally, so when it came to eating the meal I had prepared for myself, I wasn't able to savor the taste and I ended up missing the moment. Any good cook or chef will tell you that they rarely enjoy their own meals as much as the ones for whom the meals have been prepared enjoy them. Sometimes we may not be able to see how effective our deeds are, and it takes others to point out our effectiveness.

This same principle is true when it comes to dealing with women. In order to establish a solid relationship, you have to focus on doing the little things because they cumulatively build desire in a woman. If a woman finds you attractive but you do not build that desire, you'll eventually hear her say, "I need some space," or "I don't think this is going anywhere." While she may be attracted to you, she may not want to keep and claim you as her very own. At times she might appear withdrawn or even contentious with you.

When men notice these signs, they'll do something really big, hoping it will re-ignite the passion. I've known men who went as far as purchasing a vehicle for a woman, or assuming her car payments just to prove to the woman that they cared about her. I've also known guys who took their girlfriends on an all-paid exotic vacation, thinking the time spent together would do wonders and restore the fire that was lacking in the relationship. What's funny is that almost every time a single guy takes his girlfriend on an expensive vacation, they break up within a few months after returning. Now don't get me wrong, there is nothing incorrect about taking a woman on a vacation and paying for everything, but I think that's for people who have been in a long-term exclusive relationship.

If you're single and you want to go on vacation with your new girlfriend, it is best for both of you to pay for your own selves. She covers her expenses, and you do the same for yourself. The reason for this is that she won't feel pressured and obliged to do you any favors, and you as a guy, will have realistic expectations. Even if in the future the relationship falls apart, you won't resent that you spent large sums of money on her.

When two people are married, they usually have joint accounts so both parties contribute the money they spend on their vacations. It is possible for a woman to fall deeply in love with you, and she'll actually be the one spending money on you. I've never been in a relationship where the person I was dating didn't spend money on me. I have absolutely no problem paying for meals or going to fancy locations, but there are times when a woman will insist on picking up the tab. Giving is a sign that the woman you are with doesn't have a problem with greed.

You should seek relationships with women who are as willing to spend resources on you as you are on them. I want to give you the three Es that are necessary to trigger desire in a woman. They are: Energy, Enigma, and Engaging. These ingredients are what women respond to.

Energy – A positive outlook on life equates to positive energy, and because feelings have a presence, that energy will be felt by those around you. You can enter a room where two people are angry at each other and be able to sense the negative vibe, without anyone having said a word. Parents can walk into a room and instinctively tell that the kids have been doing something mischievous. Women are very intuitive by nature, so the aura you exude can easily be sensed by them, just as you can sense it when people don't want you around, without them saying anything.

For those who work in the corporate world, you can walk into your office and sense by the way the employees are acting that someone is about to be let go. The same way you're able to pick up on that vibe, is the same way women do. The key to generating this positive energy with women is to keep your problems to yourself. Never burden a woman before she becomes your girlfriend, with your problems. Focus your conversation on subjects that aren't dismal. Nobody wants to be around someone who has a negative outlook on life because such people are toxic and eventually drain you emotionally.

Many men succeed in getting a woman's number and may even make it to the first date, but wonder why she stopped returning the phone calls or keeps breaking dates. We live in a society where men are taught that it is okay to pour out your heart to a woman, because women love sensitive men. The last time I checked the divorce rate was over 50 percent. If these principles that men and women's magazines encourage you to use were effective, we would have a lower divorce rate. Women already have they own little problems. They have to worry about looking good, so every day they wake up early in the morning and spend an entire forty five minutes wearing make-up and fixing their hair just to look good for us. They then have to worry about if the clothes they are wearing make them look fat. When they leave their homes, they have to deal with the guys who are hitting on them. If that isn't enough, every month they have to deal with hormonal fluctuations caused by their period. So when a woman accepts to go on a date with you, take into consideration what she has been through to get to where she is.

When you first meet a woman, put her on a "need to know" basis. If you were an alcoholic, or drug addict in the past, or if you just lost your job, because she's on a need to know basis, she doesn't need to know. That information should be classified for the time being. It can be revealed later after you have built a solid foundation.

Your purpose is to make her your girlfriend, not your therapist. I'll assume that you are whole and well balanced, so this will not be a problem for you.

Enigma – Women love an enigma because they believe it is their God given right to know the unknown. It never ceases to amaze me when I see people on social networking Web sites revealing everything about themselves in their profiles, and sharing their private information with the whole world. I have nothing against using the Internet as a tool to communicate and keep in touch with friends, or even share photos. I just personally wouldn't use it to broadcast my life. It is better for you to let her get to know you in person, rather than read about you on some dating Web site.

If a woman finds out all about you from a Web site, what's her motivation to want to meet you in person? Why be an open book? You have destroyed the element of mystery that they are looking for. Being an enigma makes you a challenge to them and it allows them to put their natural investigative skills to work. Believe me, when you give a woman your names, the first thing she does is Google you, to see what she can come up with. When I was growing up, my mother used to check our pillowcases and closets to make sure that we didn't have material or items she didn't approve of. She was doing what women are naturally wired to do. Any time something dubious is discovered about a child, it's normally the mother who finds out; she then breaks the news to the father who had no clue about what was going in the child's life. If you're a guy reading this, I'm sure you can remember something your mother discovered that you never expected her to. You thought you had covered your tracks, but she proved you wrong.

So when you're dating a grown woman, her curiosity will drive her to want to explore who you are as a person. Don't tell a woman all about your life on the first date. Feed her that information in increments. Permit her the grace to search for and discover the diamond in the rough that you truly are. Regulate your emotions and feelings. The more she immerses herself in discovering whom you are, the more she will find you desirable, because she is investing her time in the process. She will then start to chase you. She will set up dates and call you more than you call her. Women enjoy the process of peeling off the layers, bit by bit. The thrill comes through the process of discovery. They savor every moment of the process, that's why women tend to be very spiritual, because the unknown realm is enigmatic to them.

When I was growing up, I heard a lot about witch doctors and black magic. I never really knew what that was all about. At 13 years of age, I was in Africa and I got a chance to see firsthand what all the fuss about black magic was. I remember I went to a park, and there happened to be a witch doctor performing black magic for an audience. Crowds gathered to see her act. She claimed to have healing powers and be able to cast spells. I didn't know what to think about this because this was all new to me. I watched with the rest of the crowd as she made funny faces and claimed to be speaking to the spirits. There was a man in the crowd who suddenly yelled at her, "You're a fake, your magic doesn't work." The whole crowd burst out laughing at the witch doctor. She just glanced at him and continued her show. I wasn't there for long because I was a skeptic so I left. At the end of the day, the crowd dispersed, including the man who had yelled at her. This gentleman went home that evening, played with his kids, and had dinner with his family. After tucking the kids in bed, he went to take his bath.

In Africa they tend to bathe as opposed to taking showers. His wife was in the bedroom ready to go to bed, so he went to the bathroom, shut the door, undressed, and started bathing. He lathered his hair with soap, his arms, the chest, the thighs, then all of a sudden he stopped. Something wasn't right. He felt between his thighs, and there was nothing. He looked down, and his private parts had disappeared. He released a loud cry, and jumped out of the bathtub. His wife came rushing into bathroom to find out what the commotion was all about. Her husband was wailing so loudly, the kids even woke up. She asked, "What's wrong, tell me?" Her husband replied, "I can't find my private parts." She asked, "Where did you put them?" The man answered, "I had them when I left this morning, but now they are gone."

He continued sobbing uncontrollably. This is a true story. In the meantime, the wife was looking for them all over the bathroom, but came out empty handed. She looked in all the trashcans even the fridge, and still nothing. As she was headed outside to start looking, he called her back to the bedroom and said, "I think I know who has my private parts. It's the witch doctor." She asked, "How did the witch doctor get your private parts, are you having an affair with her?" He explained to her everything that had happened during the day, and how he had disrespected her.

His wife then devised an ingenuous solution. She seemed to be more concerned about getting them back than he was. She told him to take some goats and chicken as a form of restitution, and apologize to the witch doctor for what he had said. The next day, the man loaded the goats and chickens on to a bus and went to the park the witch doctor had been performing. In Africa it is perfectly legal to carry goats, chickens, and pigs with you on a bus. To his dismay, she wasn't there. He then asked around if anybody knew where she could be found and fortunately, he was given directions.

He boarded another bus and went to witch doctor's home. When he arrived, he dropped to his knees in front of her, and with tears in his eyes, he apologized to her profusely. He said to her, "Just give me back my private parts." She felt sorry for him and accepted his gifts then told him to go back home, that everything would return to normal. Sure enough, when he arrived at his house, his package was intact. Now that's the story he told us, and anybody who has been on an African Safari will tell you that witch doctors and practitioners of black magic do indeed exist. The majority of them are women rather than men, who are drawn to that kind of spirituality. The reason, as I mentioned earlier, is because the female psyche is fascinated by the supernatural realm. At any given day in any house of worship, the women outnumber the men in attendance. It's hardwired in them to seek spirituality, whether or not they believe God exists.

I'm not saying you should conceal your identity in order to become mysterious. On your first real date with a woman, give her a reasonable amount of information and reserve the rest for the next meeting. Keep your phone calls brief and upbeat. Try not to reveal too much about yourself on the phone or using e-mail. Give her that information in person. Give her a reason to want to see you again. Don't make yourself too available because it signifies that you don't have much going in your life, and she might also think you are clingy.

Initially in the relationship, it might appear fun to be readily available, but once you become too predictable, she won't find you as desirable anymore because you are not letting her chase you. When there is a high demand for gasoline and the prices at the pump are steep, it's because the supply and the inventories are low. When there is more supply, the demand and the value of oil are low, because the market is over saturated. In other words, low demand is as a result of the oil being readily available.

It is important to note that you shouldn't play head games with her either. Return all phone calls and answer all e-mails within 24 to 48 hours. Everything you do should be free-flowing and natural. When your phone rings, answer it. Don't pretend not to have received the call in order to make her miss you. When a woman desires you, there won't be any need for you to play head games. Remember women are looking for the truth that dwells within you. That truth is a man of substance with pure intentions. Not making yourself too available isn't playing games. You had a life before you met her, so there is no need for you to put your life on hold when she's not even your girlfriend yet. Continue doing the things you were passionate about before you met her, but also schedule some time to spend with her. That's the only way your relationship will come to fruition.

Engaging – The third element necessary to trigger desire in a woman for you, is being able to engage her. That's why you have to educate yourself and be well read on current affairs. When I say educate yourself, I don't necessarily mean you have to go back to college and get a degree. I'm talking about learning something new and exciting. Find an area in your life that you are passionate about and master it. Women find knowledgeable men desirable. When you become knowledgeable and well read, it will cause women to want to take you with them to public functions because they know that you can hold an intelligent conversation with their colleagues.

One of my greatest passions is travel, however, I know that in order to enjoy and mingle with the various cultures I encounter during my travels, I have to learn a few more languages, so I am multilingual. The ability to speak a foreign language immediately puts you ahead because you have elevated your means of communicating. Your passion may not be travel. It may be the justice system. Acquire as much knowledge as possible in that area so that when you speak, you'll be an authority on that subject. The more knowledge you acquire, the more confident you'll become and you'll also become more engaging. You'll be able to explain matters that seem complex, in a very simple and understandable way. The woman you are with will be so proud to associate herself with you. Don't flaunt your knowledge in an effort to show off. The knowledge will emanate naturally in your conversations. Your vocabulary will be different from the average person. You'll learn metaphors that you can use to your advantage.

Use real life experiences to explain or make a point during a conversation. Remember not to talk too much about yourself; she might think you're bragging. Don't pretend to have all the answers. If you do not know the answer to something, have the humility to admit so. Your humility will be viewed as strength.

I would like to give you a few tips on how to be engaging.

1. Learn to become a great conversationalist. You do that by talking about things of substance. Gossiping and bad-mouthing others will diminish your standing with women because those types of conversations have no depth. I developed my conversational skills as a child, when my parents played a role reversal with me. Instead of them telling me a bedtime story before I went to bed, they made me tell them a bedtime story. Every night I had a different story for them, and as I matured, my stories reflected more of what I had experienced in life, as opposed to the fairy tales I told when I was a child. The same will happen to you if you're observant. That's why I emphasize sharing an observation with a woman when you first meet her. That's the easiest way to develop your conversational skills because they pertain to real time and real life events.

2. When you're speaking, maintain eye contact and include gestures to complement what you're saying. Politicians are very good at this. They know that in order for the audience to be able to relate to them, they have use gestures to make the connection. That's what you should do during and after your conversation. You need to establish a connection with the woman you are interested in. Think about people who use sign language to communicate. They only use gestures to convey their messages. If you can combine the spoken word with the unspoken, imagine how much more effective you will become in engaging your mate.

3.   Listen attentively. After you speak, allow the woman to respond without interrupting her. Try not to dominate the conversation, but give her a chance to state her viewpoint or observations. Most people only stay silent because they can't wait for the speaker to finish so they can speak too. Just because someone hears what you say doesn't mean they are listening attentively. While listening, try to be objective even when she reveals information about herself that might shock you. When women are unfaithful, they will normally cheat with the guy who is willing to listen to them. It's because they are slowly building a bond together. The same applies to men too. There are times when married men will go into a bar and pour their hearts out to the bartender, because their wives aren't willing to listen to them without being critical. All the bartender has to do is act like she feels his pain, and a connection will be established. The result is he'll either give her a big tip, or ask for her phone number.

4. Mention her name every once in a while as you talk to her. The most beautiful sound to anybody is the sound of his or her name. Sales people understand this and use this principle effectively to connect to customers. Find out about her interests, her goals, dreams, and aspirations. Get to know her hopes and fears and avoid talking about your accomplishments. Let her discover them as the relationship progresses. People who are highly accomplished don't feel the need to advertise their accomplishments or conquests in order to raise their status. One thing I have learned is that no amount of money can buy class. Having class is an upbringing that becomes a state of mind, and eventually a way of life. A person with class doesn't have to wear a suit and tie, or drive a Mercedes to appear classy. They can wear a simple white T-shirt and a clean pair of jeans, and still convey class. The suit and tie and Mercedes still help.

Dave Roper retold a story about African slaves who were brought to America and were being auctioned off to slave masters. As the bidding was happening, one of the slave masters turned to the auctioneer and inquired about a particular slave. The slave carried himself with such confidence and poise. He seemed unperturbed while all the other slaves were disoriented because they were being auctioned off. The slave master said to the auctioneer, "That slave over there, I notice there is something different about him." To which the auctioneer replied, "Back in Africa, he was a prince, and he hasn't forgotten it."

5. Don't wear out your welcome. Disengage from the conversation after an appropriate amount of time. She will want to hear from you, and see you again. That's the reason I am against using e-mails and text messages to build a relationship while it is still in its infancy. I also don't care for online dating because communication is in a virtual world. The dating experience should be empirical... something you can see, feel, touch, hear or smell. I believe if you're socially calibrated, you should have the skills to meet a live human being and interact with them in the real world, instead of interacting in cyberspace. After all, you will eventually have to meet the person you've been communicating with electronically in person. Why not just develop social skills to meet new people. Find events that are happening in your city. Go to a movie by yourself, you never know whom you'll meet. Take cooking lessons or join a local club. Choose activities that will allow you to build your social skills and expand your circle of friends. Make it a point to make one new friend a month. At the end of the year, you'll have twelve new friends.

As you work on your inner man, you will out-grow most of your old friends. Some of them are people who have no ambitions of expanding their horizons. Others might be people at your workplace who are satisfied with their entry-level positions they have had for several years, yet you probably dream of starting your own business. Whatever the case is, your self-improvement will be evident, and the mediocre bystanders will interpret your confidence as arrogance. Your dreams and ambitions will become an irritation to them. This is because the new you is no longer a follower of the crowd, but has evolved into a trailblazer.

Some reading this might be shocked and say, "What about money? What about looks? Aren't those important to women too?" Those are important to women, but if you are a practitioner of the natural approach, you will have already worked on your inner game, your health habits, your appearance, and you will be expanding your horizons. Your inner beauty will manifest itself through your personality, ambitions, goals, and passion. Those qualities will be enough to nullify what you lack in the looks department, and will prove to a woman that you have the desire to succeed in life. So even if you're not the best looking guy, or richest kid on the block, your state of mind, personality, knowledge base, and passion will be your greatest assets.

Believe it or not, a quality woman enjoys watching her man grow and achieve his dreams. Women are nurturers by nature, and even if you are struggling, but are making an effort to achieve your goals, quality women will give the relationship a chance. Gold-diggers will dump you in a heartbeat for a bigger better deal, because someone lied to them that the grass is always greener on the other side. A quality woman has a strong work ethic and knows that even the greatest monuments, were built one brick at a time until they became national treasures. When she invests her time and encouragement in you during your growth process, she will never leave you because your successes have now become hers. Those are the women who make the most loyal girlfriends or wives, because they were with you when all you had was a dream, and the only thing you had going for you was your passion. Even a woman who is richissima and makes more money than her guy, will not mind being in a relationship with him as long as he exhibits passion to get ahead in life.

After the first date, if you have played your cards right, there won't be any need for a quality woman to flake on you. She will call you when she says she will call, and on all subsequent dates, she will arrive promptly. She will make an effort to set aside some time for both of you to have some privacy. A woman who is interested in you will not want to bring her friends along on a date or give you ambiguous answers about her availability for a particular event you've scheduled for the two of you. I mentioned earlier that the small things you do will have a profound effect on her, so avoid buying expensive gifts before you are sure that she's yours exclusively. The greatest gift you should give her is the gift of your time. Other gifts you can give her during the initial phase of dating are: the gift of humor, your understanding, the gift of patience, and also the gift of kindness.

I remember in the mid-nineties I was in New Mexico and received a letter from one of my sisters. She informed me that she was engaged and was planning to get married. I continued to read the letter hoping she would list tangible qualities about the man she was about to marry, but none were mentioned. She emphasized that his kindness was one of the most important things about him she was drawn to. I had never thought of kindness as being paramount to a woman's needs. I wondered how it could be that kindness was one of the decisive factors women considered in choosing a man. It was then that I started to dissect our upbringing. I concluded that women who have a loving and kind father, tend to choose a mate with those qualities. A woman knows if you are kind to her, you will also be kind to the children you have together. No woman wants her children abandoned, so an emotionally sound woman values a man who demonstrates kindness to her. The father-daughter relationship also decides how women perceive men. Two of the most important ingredients for a woman in a relationship are the need to feel secure, and the need to feel relevant. Your kindness and understanding will instill that in her. She wants to know that you value her opinions and take her seriously. When you demonstrate that, she will find your persona relatable because she uses her father's persona as a reference point. That's the reason why grown women refer to their husbands as "Daddy." To this very day, my mother still refers to my father as "Daddy." It's not unusual for her to say, "Don't forget to get Daddy a Christmas gift," and so on.

I'm from the Generation-X, and we have a phrase we commonly use. When we are in a relationship with a woman, and everything is going well, we'll turn to the girl and ask her, "Who's your Daddy?" She gets it. She'll reply that you're her Daddy. Spanish women prefer to use the phrase "Papi." She's knows you're not trying to take her biological father's place. You're just trying to be endearing. That only happens when you extend kindness to a woman in a relationship.

There are practitioners in the field of psychology who say that the two most important things to a woman in a relationship are affection and communication. I beg to differ with my contemporaries. My personal research on the frontlines of the dating scene, has shown that it is not affection and communication that are most important to women; it is the need to feel valued and relevant in a relationship. My findings are from women who are clinically sane and emotionally sound. Even prostitutes and strippers get a lot of affection and communication from their clients but are still empty on the inside. Nowhere was that captured better as it was in the movie *Pretty Woman* when Vivienne, played by Julia Roberts went shopping in a posh neighborhood and was devalued by the owners of the store because of her appearance. The same happened to her when Richard Gere's lawyer played by Jason Alexander tried to force himself on her. All she ever wanted was to feel valued and relevant as a human being. Richard Gere understood that well, so he took her on a shopping spree and instructed the store owners to take care of her, and they made her feel valued, but he also made her feel relevant when his lawyer called him and he ended the phone call briefly after talking to him when he said he was in the middle of a very important conversation. Gere made Vivienne his priority, which in return made her feel relevant.

It is possible however, to feel valued and not feel relevant. For example, your company or institution you work for might consider you to be a valuable employee and even invite you to attend corporate meetings. Nevertheless, if they never ask for your input or ideas, even though you may feel valued by them, you won't feel relevant because your ideas seem to be unimportant to them. It is therefore important that you not only make a woman feel valued, but also relevant. Ask her for her input on important decisions or ask for suggestions and opinions. Value her with your time and the way your treat and talk to her. A woman who feels valued and relevant in a relationship is receiving affection and communication. I would argue with people in the psychology community that, what is the use of a woman receiving affection and communication, but is devalued and feels irrelevant in the relationship? That's why I used the analogy of prostitutes who receive affection and communication, but at the end of the day they don't feel valued. Affection and communication are a byproduct of a relationship where a woman feels valued and relevant.

If she's a single mother, she wants you to show her child or children the same kindness you would your very own. Physical gifts should be given only on special occasions like birthdays or Christmas, until she becomes your girlfriend or wife. After that, you can give them as pleasant surprises, but don't overdo it, because if she gets too used to receiving gifts from you, they will lose their ability to affect her on an emotional level.

When I was at the Vatican, in Vatican City on April 5 2006, I decided to visit the numerous Vatican museums. I took several pictures with my digital camera, and also video footage of artwork dating back to the Renaissance. Among the pictures I took were the famous paintings by Raphael for Pope Julius II's apartment called The Disputation and The School of Athens. As I proceeded to the Sistine chapel with both cameras still turned on, one of the palace guards told me I couldn't take pictures once I entered the Sistine chapel. I couldn't understand why they would let me take photos of paintings in the rest of the Vatican palace and not the Sistine chapel. This chapel has the ceiling paintings or frescoes of Michelangelo's Creation and Last Judgment. Italians understand that a treasure is bound to lose its value due to overexposure. That's the reason they are restrictive when it comes to certain artistic pieces they value.

The same applies to relationships and the frequency at which gifts are given. Give them sparingly if you really want a woman to value your gifts. You also have to be sensualissimo when you are with her, and come up with creative romantic ideas in order to keep her from getting bored in the relationship.

I do have a word of caution regarding kindness. Kindness is different from being nice. Some men are too nice to women and they think that translates to kindness. You do not have to be nice to be kind. As a matter of fact being too nice will work against you, because you'll seem as though you are trying to gain her approval. By kindness I mean being affectionate and having empathy at the same time. You have the other person's best interests at heart. Being nice is a superficial way one person may act if that person wishes to receive a favor from another. That's the reason why if a woman defines you as being nice, chances are, she doesn't think that you are boyfriend material, and you'll end up just being her buddy. You're are not looking for a friend-girl, you are looking for a girlfriend. I therefore do not advocate being too nice; instead, show kindness to the woman you're interested in. It is better for you to be described as 'kind' by a woman you are courting, than 'nice.'

Chapter 3

Mistakes to Avoid

One bad relationship can ruin your entire life.

- *e*Nigma

Pinpointing the mistakes you've made in the past that ruined your relationships with quality women, can be a window into what not to do in the future. Let's assume that you have learned from your past mistakes. Since nobody is perfect, I have a few practical guidelines that will help you enjoy fulfilling and healthy relationships. You may not currently be in a relationship, and that's okay. There is nothing wrong with being unattached as you wait for the quality woman you truly deserve.

When you have a medical problem, you'll seek out the doctor most qualified to treat you. You'll do your homework to make sure that you don't end up being treated by someone with questionable credentials or medical practices. You should have the same mentality when it comes to women. You have to be choosy when it comes to whom you let get close to you because one bad relationship can ruin your entire life. It is very important that you screen the women you let into your world, just as they screen men.

1. Avoid pursuing relationships with women who cannot handle money responsibly. The way a person handles money can tell you a lot about that person. A woman who gets herself in excessive debt symbolizes someone who has a problem with greed. They seek to possess more than they can afford. There is what I call reasonable debt which includes, a mortgage, car notes, college loans, and other expenses that people wouldn't normally be able to pay cash for. However, if a woman is spending more money than she actually earns, she has a greed problem. It takes maturity to create a budget. The purpose of a budget is to regulate a person's spending habits. A budget allows one to determine what one can or cannot afford. It creates discipline in one's life.

If you attach yourself to a woman who is a spendthrift, you may eventually find yourself in financial dire straits. The expensive dinners, vacations, jewelry, and other finer things in life, will take a financial toll on your wallet. You have to prioritize your spending. The things that are of great importance should be on the top of your list. If for instance you plan to go to an expensive restaurant on a Sunday afternoon, but the Tuesday before that you receive your utility bill, pay off your bill first. It is more of a priority than the dinner, which is a mere luxury.

I have absolutely no problem with spending money on a woman you are dating, because giving is a byproduct of love. You must spend within your means, and not accumulate debt in order to impress a woman. Don't be afraid to tell a woman that you can't afford to take her to a certain restaurant. A quality woman knows that money doesn't grow on trees and she might even suggest having a picnic in a park instead. There are a lot of hardworking women who live in a reality where they work hard for everything they have. They do not have a sense of entitlement, nor would they hold it against you if you prioritize your spending. Those are the women you should seek out. I personally know men whose credit was ruined or who came to near bankruptcy, because they got involved with the wrong type of women. If you overlook a woman's careless spending habits while you are still dating, and you do decide to marry her and have joint accounts or hand her the checkbook, those habits will even magnify themselves more after you are married. You will be responsible for cleaning up the financial mess if you are the primary breadwinner. So it is very important to go into any relationship with your eyes open.

2. When a woman tells you she is not interested in having a relationship with you, don't pressure her into one, and don't take it personally either. If you have done everything right in the approach and your presentation, but she still doesn't want a relationship, simply tell yourself that she has bad judgment, and pursue someone else. In your eyes, a woman with good judgment would notice your value, but since the one you are interested in doesn't notice it, why continue to waste your precious time on someone who doesn't want you in her life?

A woman who finds you desirable will be eager to enter a relationship with you. If she's bold enough, she'll even go as far as proposing to you at some point in the relationship. I'm speaking out of experience. She will encourage your advances and ask for exclusivity. As a man of quality yourself, you should be interacting with several women and gather as many phone numbers as possible so you can have a diverse and large pool, from which to choose. You have to be selective with your choices and screen those you let in your life. Women screen every man they encounter. They can't just embrace anyone who spits a good game. They screen for authenticity.

A woman who is a fake will naturally draw fake men to herself. All her girlfriends will also be fake and she won't be able to discern you if you're authentic. She will be more comfortable around people like her because she's afraid if she's in the presence of people who are genuine, they will be able to see through her façade. Amazingly, these women also have the propensity to enter fake marriages, for purpose of convenience. Sometimes it is a blessing in disguise if a woman tells you she's not interested. Life might be trying to save you from some impending doom, so don't act like it's the end of the world when you run into a brick wall.

One day when I was six years old, my father picked my siblings and me up from school at lunchtime as he usually did. There was something he had purchased, and on the way back home, he asked us to try and guess what it was. We all tried guessing, from a brand new television, to a new car, a new music system, but none of us was able guess correctly. He said he wouldn't tell us because he wanted us to see it for ourselves, which even made us more excited. When we arrived, he drove around to the backyard, and we saw a huge German shepherd chained to a tree. From then on we raised German shepherds, but they were all hand picked by him.

When I was fourteen years old, I asked him if I could have my very own handpicked puppy. My Dad didn't see any need in us getting another dog, so he kept saying no to me. I continued to pester him for months until one day he agreed to take me to the dog pound. I believe the reason my father bought me a puppy was not because we lacked guard dogs, but because I wore him out. Now parents naturally want their kids to have good things, and as long as it made me happy to have this puppy, my Dad was happy too because I was his son.

Relationships with women don't work that way. A woman you are pursuing is not related to you so she's not obligated to you in any way. Some men think by persistently pressing a woman into changing her mind, she will eventually give in, but that's not necessarily true. There are some women who will succumb and actually end up dating guys who pressure them. These women, however, tend to be driven by loneliness. Some women think they always have to be in a relationship in order to feel wholesome, so they'll date men they aren't even attracted to or find desirable, in an effort to overcome their loneliness. Those types of relationships tend to be short lived and end disastrously because there was no solid foundation that was built in the beginning.

An emotionally sound woman will not strip herself of her dignity by settling for less than she believes she deserves. Women are naturally meant to be kind, so they tend to be polite when brushing off a man. A woman's lack of interest in you will manifest itself in several ways. If you call a woman and leave a message on her answering machine or send her an e-mail and she doesn't respond, she's sending you a subliminal message that she doesn't desire or value you. If you invite her to a social event and she turns down your invitation, or accepts it but then flakes on you, she's simply saying to you indirectly, that she doesn't value you enough as a human being, to want to spend her time with you.

A flake is a woman who doesn't honor her word, and will break an appointment without any explanation or consideration for the other party. Flakes aren't just limited to the dating community. They exist in all areas of life. I'm sure you know some people you would never do business with because they are undependable and unreliable. They don't value other people's time and are unreasonable. In the dating community, women only flake on the men they do not desire. If a woman desires a man, she'll do whatever is necessary, just to spend time with him.

As a man of high quality, you have to know when to back off. I currently know a woman who is going nuts because a certain gentleman showed interest in her and she played hard to get for several months, but now he's no longer interested in her. Both of these people are in their mid-fifties and divorced. After a while, the gentleman did the honorable thing and backed off due to her lack of reciprocation. The woman didn't hear from him for several weeks so she decided to contact him. She is now the one pursuing him. At the time she contacted him, his interest in her had plummeted and was reluctant to even go out with her. In the meantime, the woman's passion for him grew so intense, within two months she was even thinking of marriage. She doesn't seem to understand why he isn't pursuing her as he once did, and it is driving her bananas. Remember, this is the same guy she rejected when he showed interest in her, but now that he's playing it cool and has backed away, she's stressing.

3. A woman who repeatedly degrades or belittles men in her conversations is someone you should seriously consider avoiding. In your search for a stable relationship, you have to keep reminding yourself that it is a quality woman you are looking for. You really aren't going to find quality women frequenting bars and clubs, so you have to practice approaching women during the day. Practically all the women I've been in relationships with, I met them during the day, and all were sober.

Quality women do of course go out dancing and to other social events because women are naturally social beings. However, women of quality go clubbing once in a very blue moon, and when they go out, they go specifically to have fun and not to find a man. They tend to prefer to socialize at family oriented events or throw their own house parties because they have a certain level of control over that type of atmosphere and their reality. These women know that their reputations depend on the image they portray, and will be pre-judged based on their associations. The one distinct factor that sets a quality woman apart, is that she doesn't feel the need to degrade men in order to validate herself. She won't act like she is doing you a favor by giving you company. She loves manly men and is proud to be associated with them. These women don't misinterpret manliness for sexism or chauvinism.

One of the saddest things that happened to men was the invention of the metro sexual. A metro sexual is simply a man who is apologetic about his manliness. Men are so afraid to embrace their manliness, some even have to ask the women they are dating or married to for permission to do the things they were passionate about when they were still single. When you are in the presence of a woman who has nothing kind to say about men in general, what makes you think she will treat you any better? A lot of them have been wounded and it's their pain that's speaking. As a result, when some men are in the presence of women who bad-mouth other men, but want to win their favor, they will abandon their manly traits in order to appear more acceptable to the women they are pursing. They'll even wear clothing with soft feminine colors like pink, in an effort to appear non-threatening to women.

You rarely see women apologize for their femininity. That's why they are not ashamed to wear makeup in the middle of busy traffic. It's dangerous to do but all women have an impulse to look attractive. Let us dissect the purpose of makeup. Women rub something called 'blush' on their cheeks, and wear red lipstick to signify that they are fertile and full of life. Even those that are post-menopausal want to feel the same. Since blood is the life of every living creature, the redness on the cheeks and lips is meant to create an illusion that they're full of life. They'll even wear the make up right in front of you, and create this illusion before your very own eyes. Now any magician or illusionist will never reveal to you the way they create their illusions, but don't tell that to women. The truth is, guys don't really care, because women are just doing what they do.

The reason I mention seeing man bashing as a red flag is because I've seen many men, whose reputations were destroyed by false allegations. I've known men who lost custody of their kids because of one false accusation by the woman who bore the children. That's the reason why if you're on a college campus at a fraternity party, or a single guy building a career, and you're at a social event, you have to regulate your conduct for the sake of your reputation. It may not be a social setting. You might be in a position of power and influence in the corporate arena or marketplace. Refrain from using intimidation to take advantage of the women you have access to. The problem with using intimidation is that eventually, its cousin named manipulation, will come back to haunt you. Intimidation is when a person in a position of power tries to control a person of less power, using fear tactics. Manipulation is when the person in a position of less power, tries to control the person in a position of influence.

4. If you are interested in having a committed and exclusive relationship, avoid a relationship with a woman who tells you that their careers are the most important thing to them than anything else. It is possible for a woman to have a successful career and a fulfilling relationship or marriage, if she is well balanced. I greatly admire women who can raise multiple kids and also sustain a career. My mother was one of them. She had seven children, but both she and my dad had careers. The reason why certain women are able to have a fulfilling relationship and career at the same time is because they value their family most. Despite her hectic career, my mother made two home cooked meals everyday – Breakfast and supper. She did this until my sisters were old enough to cook. Even still, she at least cooked the main course, and let my sisters prepare the side dishes.

Any person who places his or her career above family or loved ones, clearly does not take other people seriously or value them.

Such a person lives a subjective life as opposed to an objective one. You will find yourself very unfulfilled if you ignore the words of a woman who tells you that her career is what she values the most. Such people feel guilty when they take time off from work, and don't know how to relax on vacations. They feel the need to take their work with them wherever they go, and are constantly working on job related projects instead of enjoying their vacations.

When a woman tells you that her career is the most important thing to her, she is very serious. Don't take her words lightly. You will never be number one in her life. Her family and friends will never be number one in her life. If you marry such a woman and have children with her, they will turn out to be detached and withdrawn because they never really bonded with their mother during the first few years of life. She will value her work more than her children or husband. You and the children will become burdensome because she will feel that you are holding her back from achieving more in life.

Life is about sacrifices and you have to know what is the most important thing in your life. That's where you will focus most of your energy. I often see men or hear from guys who feel abandoned in their marriages or relationships. These relationships are loveless and dry because the men failed to heed the red flag when the women told them that their careers were more important than anything else. Somehow these men thought that the women they married would change with time but it didn't happen.

Anytime you see a single father who has full custody of his children it most likely is because the mother of the children was willing to walk away from the relationship and abandon her very own children. That's what happens when women value their families less than their careers. They will walk out on you in a heartbeat if they were given the choice to either spend time at the office or with their loved ones.

I believe when people are on their deathbeds, during the last few hours before they die, they are not saying to themselves, "I wish I had spent more time working at the office, or neglecting my family." When people are on their deathbeds, they are saying to themselves,

"I wish I had slowed down and spent more time with my family. I wish I had taken more time off from work and demonstrated to my spouse and children how important they were to me."

Children abandoned by parents during childhood, tend not to value their father and mother once the parents become senior citizens. Just as a parent can abandon the child during his or her childhood because that parent is too busy with work, it's my personal opinion that the same behavior is transferred to the child through impartation. So when the parents get older, these children will prematurely put them in nursing homes because the parent or parents demonstrated to the children that work was more important than family. I suspect that when you go to nursing homes, the elderly who rarely receive phone calls or visitors are the ones who never valued people and relationships, while they were young and healthy. The elderly who receive the most guests and phone calls, are the ones who valued friends and family over work.

My personal belief is that children should take care of their aging parents unless it is the parent's request, or medically to the parent's advantage to be in a healthcare facility. Parents should spend their closing years in honor and dignity.

A woman whose career is the most important thing to her will be void of emotion. She might be physically present with you, but far away in her thoughts. You won't have a romantic bond that creates chemistry. The relationship will seem mechanical, because she doesn't know how to savor the moments you spend together. Women who value their work more than their loved ones tend to make the most horrible girlfriends and I suspect the worst wives. If you are married to one, you better pray that you never end up in a hospital's emergency room on life support. You can put two and two together and figure out what she's likely to tell the doctor, if he or she asks her whether or not to continue the life support. She most likely will not want to be bothered by the mere thought of having to take care of you and making hospital visits on a regular basis, because you are taking up her valuable time. While you're in pain, she'll be more concerned about closing the next deal, or traveling on the next business trip. Those women tend to be the most unfulfilled and have the least friends they can count on. You can never use work as a replacement for the lack of inner joy. You do not live to work, you work to live. The purpose of work is to help you sustain a living, not to rob you of the simple pleasures of living life.

In May 2002, I received an E-mail from a friend. When I opened the e-mail, there was a hyperlink enclosed. I clicked on it and it led me to a Web site. I can't really remember the content of the Web site, but I remember that it had a piece of poetry by an unknown author. I t was a long piece of writing, but the words that stood out are still imprinted on my mind. It had to do with a man who had a dream that he had a chance to ask God questions about mankind. One of the questions he asked God was, "What surprises you most about mankind?" To which God replied, "That they lose their health in pursuit of wealth, and then use their wealth to try and restore their health. That they live as though they will never die, and die as though they had never lived." Out of all the words I read, those are the ones that still resonate within me. Having a successful career or loving your work isn't bad, as long as you have balance that creates a well-rounded individual. Don't be a slave to your career. Live a little.

5. Avoid committing yourself to a woman who has addictions she refuses to acknowledge and seek help for. It could be drugs, alcohol, the club scene, living life in the fast lane, or any other form of addiction. Whatever it may be, it is always easier for the person with the addictive habit to pull you down to their level, than it is for you to lift them up to your level. Some men will compromise their ethics, simply to demonstrate their loyalty the woman they are try-ing to impress. Addictions aren't always obvious. If you are new to relationships, it is possible to be involved with someone and not know that the person leads a double life. Sometimes a man might already be in too deep. You have to ask yourself how her behavior might affect not just the relationship, but also you. Are you willing to go to jail for that person? Is it worth it? If you have been think-ing of marrying that person but have only recently discovered the addictions they were hiding from you, is that the person you want to raise your children? Would you be proud to introduce that person as your wife or girlfriend? Out of over 3 billion women on the planet, do you feel she's the best for you?

Now turn the tables around for a second. If you were the one struggling with the addictions, do you think she would want to build a future with you, or would she leave you for someone more reputable? These are questions you have to ask yourself before committing to an exclusive relationship. If you truly care about this person, rather than abandon her, advise her to seek help or counseling. If she's in denial about her problem, then you won't be able to help her. A person has to admit he or she has a problem before you can help them.

There are certain addictions that don't involve substances. A woman can be addicted to her past boyfriends. It gives some women a sense of validation knowing that they can go back and win their ex. For this reason, even though a woman might be in a relationship, she could still have contact with her ex boyfriend, especially if he was the one who ended the relationship. Some men can deal with a woman meeting for lunch every once in a while with an ex, but if you want to be exclusive with a woman and she insists of keeping in contact with the men from her past, you will have a serious problem when your relationship starts to falter. The men she's in touch with will give her a shoulder to cry on, and because she will have known them longer than she has known you, she's more likely to fall back on any one of them during a moment of vulnerability.

With all the diseases going around, you should not have to take these kinds of risks by sharing the affection of one woman with several other guys. Dating her will be like playing the NFL. Too many players, and all are after one thing…to score. If you're at point in the relationship and you feel your are ready to settle down with the woman you are dating, but she refuses to let go of her past relationships, then you are dealing with potentially disrespectful woman. She has to have enough respect for you to be willing to walk away from her past boyfriends so she can give your relationship a chance to flourish.

I want to give you a word of caution though. When faced with a situation like this, don't act in a jealous way or give her ultimatums.

She will resent you for that. Simply state how her actions make you feel, and ask her what her response would be if you were the one doing what she's doing. If she continues to act in a belligerent or unreasonable way, and ignores your pleas, dump her. She will never change. She disqualified herself for your love and affection, and perhaps the pain of losing you will be her greatest teacher. Never take back a woman who blatantly disrespects you, because that is a sign that she has emotional or psychological problems that she needs to resolve on her own. That's how tough love works. You're a man of quality and the purpose of this book is to help you identify quality women that deserve your attention.

6. Never pursue a serious relationship with a woman who despises the type of work you do. If a woman doesn't think your line of work is honorable, she will begin to look down on you, and to some extent convince herself that she's doing you a favor by being with you. Some women fall in love with the kind of job a man has, as opposed to who he truly is as a human being. You might currently be in pursuit of a woman, and wonder why she stopped her reciprocation to you after you told her what you did for a living. The reason is because she has defined you based on the type of work you do. The way a woman talks to and treats an investment banker is different from the way she treats a janitor. Both professions are honorable, but if she perceives your job to be inferior, she will think that you are inferior to her too because she won't be able to brag about you to her friends or family. She wonders to herself how she'll introduce you to her colleagues at her company's annual Christmas party, or at other social events, so it will be very hard for her to view you with honor if she doesn't think your job is honorable. I believe that's why men make up fancy job titles when women ask them what they do.

A woman instinctively views the measure of a man based on his potential as a provider. The more prestigious his job is, the better a provider he appears, in her eyes. Your earning power is directly proportional to how seriously a woman will regard you as a potential mate. That's the reason why at the beginning of the book, in chapter one, I encourage you to improve every aspects of your life, and have something you strive for. That small adjustment in your life will solve this little problem for you. The energy you exude while pursuing your aspirations will be enough to cause any quality woman to recognize your potential, and take you seriously.

In October 2005, I was in Rome taking some video footage of one of Rome's most famous streets called Via Veneto. It was made famous because scenes from the movie La Dolce Vita [The Sweet Life] with Marcello Mastroianni were filmed on that particular street. As I walked toward Piazza Barberini, I was greeted by a gentleman named Luca, who thought I was from Jamaica because of my dreads. He started telling me about the history of the monuments and recommended certain hot spots to me, that he insisted I needed to visit to fully enjoy the part of Rome I was staying. After the brief conversation we had, he beamed with such pride and told me that he was so happy he had found a job that very same day. I asked him what job it was and he replied that he was a waiter at the café next to where we were standing. I had never seen someone display such pride about a job as simple as waiting tables. As I was leaving the vicinity I learned a very good lesson. No matter how simplistic your profession may be, if you do it with passion and excellence, people will always value who you are. You will become a source of inspiration to them. Those who take their jobs for granted will be reminded of how fortunate they are to have employers who afford them the right to earn a living. As for those women who despise your job, simply dismiss them as both narrow minded and shallow, and never cater to their arrogance.

According to Tom Mortensen a senior scholar at The Pell Institute for the Study of Opportunity in Higher Education, women outnumber men in college graduates. The U.S. Census Bureau also shows the number of females enrolling in college after high school increased by 20 percent, from 1967 to 2000 while the number of men has decreased by four percent. Because women graduate in far greater numbers than men from college campuses, you will meet several women who are more educated than you, or those who outearn you.

When you are courting such a woman, don't feel intimidated by her status in life. There are some men who feel the need to put down women who are more successful than they are. You work against yourself when you do that because it translates to insecurity on your behalf. Women consider insecure men to be weak, and you'll never stand a chance with a woman if you continue to belittle her for the successes she earned.

Instead of putting her down, if she informs you she was just promoted at work, congratulate her, and you will both experience a rewarding relationship. However, there is a small percentage of women who might hold prestigious jobs or have greater earning power than the men they are involved with, and feel the need to rub it in their faces. What they are psychologically trying to do is make the men feel less of a man, so they can be less threatening to the women's careers. If you ever get involved with such a woman, she will view you as her competition rather than her boyfriend. She will compete with you in everything you do, just to prove to you that she is able. If you buy a glass coffee table, she'll buy herself a marble one. If you mention you've traveled to a certain locale, she'll mention that she's vacationed at a fancier or more expensive place. The relationship will not be genuine, because she'll always try to find ways to prove that she's better than you, or be defiant and contentious with you. You should call such a woman out on that kind of behavior. If you don't, the result will be endless arguments that will eventually cause the demise of the relationship.

In the summer of 1998, I was in Clovis, New Mexico. A friend of mine had a girlfriend he was madly in love with. She was more educated and successful than he was. The relationship was very troubled and was filled with arguments. His problem was that when he was angry, he would belittle her about the things she had confided in him. One night they had such a big fight, she called the relationship off, and decided to move back into her parent's home. Because my friend had to go to work the next day, his soon-to-be ex-girlfriend woke up early and prepared him lunch. She then packed her bags and left without saying goodbye to him. When he awoke, he found a note on next to the meal that simply said, "Your Lunch." During his lunch break, he drove to my place and told me that his girlfriend had left him, which wasn't a surprise to me. He then offered me half his lunch. I was very suspicious about his sudden generosity so I asked him why he was being so benevolent toward me. His exact words were, "My girlfriend broke up with me out of anger. Before she left, she cooked for me this meal, and said it was my lunch. I am offering you part of it because I want to wait until you have eaten your half. If nothing happens to you, then I'll know it's safe for me to eat my half." Can you believe this cat? He actually wanted me to be his guinea pig. That's nerve, right there. I politely turned down his meal, which he ended up disposing of in a nearby trashcan. His constant belittling of her caused the relationship to fall apart.

A woman who values you will never try to make you feel less of a man than you really are because she's more educated or makes more than you. She'll always be willing to reach out to you, if you celebrate her achievements and provide encouragement when she needs it. Everybody successful has experienced some sort of failure, while pursuing his or her dreams. Never reveal information that a woman confides in you in private. You will become more and more desirable to her, because she has finally found someone who embraces her along with her successes, and previous failures.

7. Never try to mend a broken heart. Frankly, some broken hearts may never mend. If a woman has previously been in a relationship that involved abuse of any kind, her self-image may be damaged beyond repair. You cannot unscramble the eggs. Men naturally want to repair or fix anything that is broken. The biggest mistake that men make is to think that in their own strength they can restore a woman's badly damaged self-worth, or even help her overcome a broken heart. Even therapists and psychiatrists resort to prescribing medications that simply treat the symptoms and ignore the causes.

No amount of human love can cause a broken heart to heal. Unlike a physical wound that heals when left alone, an emotional wound is different. I have observed people who confessed that they had recovered from the pain of their past failed relationships, but for some strange reason, they seemed to still harbor hostility toward the person they were involved with. What generates this hostility is a very powerful feature we all possess called memory. The purpose of memory is to retrieve past experiences whether good or bad. I have come to the conclusion that people tend to harbor bitterness toward others who have wronged them, not because they are unforgiving, but because the frequency at which they retrieve and replay their bad experiences, outweighs the frequency at which they retrieve and re-play the delightful experiences. By constantly replaying these nega-tive experiences, the mind creates the impression of an emotional wound that is incurable. This then translates into heartache. So a lot of people will go on medication to temporarily relieve themselves of this heartache, and fail to address the root cause.

On a side note, I am not against therapy or medication, I just believe before one considers that option, one should take a good inventory of oneself, and find out why one feels the way one feels. Reframing the mind can be a starting point. To reframe the mind means switching the frequency of negative recall, to more positive recall. It does not mean being in denial. I've never met anyone who grew richer, healthier or prettier by worrying or dwelling upon past negative experiences. However, I've seen people grow wealthier, and even appear to be youthfully rejuvenated by recalling the posi-tive experiences. This is how wonderfully the mind wired: Heart-ache and disappointment are inevitable, so the mind has a weapon to neutralize these negative factors. It's called creative imagina-tion. Creativity allows us to use the past or present positive experi-ences as a stepping-stone to thrust us into our desired future. There are times in life when we might go through intense hardships and eventually overcome them. As time goes by, we might encounter more hardships, so we recall the moments when we overcame the previous hardships, and say to ourselves, "If I could weather those past hardships and come out victorious with my sanity intact, I can overcome the current crisis I am facing." The mind will then find creative ways to accomplish the desired future using your creative imagination. It is the process of creativity that causes the mind to rejuvenate which manifests itself through a new outlook on life, and a desire to succeed in one's endeavors.

The same is true for relationships. The person with the emotional wounds has to want to be whole. If your desire to see a woman heal emotionally exceeds her desire to be healed, all your efforts will be in vain, especially if the woman's emotional pain was as a result of betrayal. As a matter of fact, you will appear to be the bad guy, despite your efforts to help her overcome her baggage. The reason you will be blamed even though you do things out of the goodness of your heart to see the person heal is because, people who have been betrayed, tend to stereotype an entire segment of the population. Ask anybody who's experienced identity theft Online. They will tell you that they don't shop online because one merchant was dishonest while handling their financial information.

Trust is something that can almost never be restored or earned with people who have been betrayed. In such a relationship, even though you are loyal and faithful, every time she calls you and gets your voicemail, she immediately thinks you are with somebody else. If you smile at a waitress during a dinner date, or receive an innocent phone call from a female colleague, a woman who's been betrayed will think you have your eye on the other woman. Behavioral scientists David, Stanley, and Derald Wing Sue refer to this as "arbitrary inference", in their book Understanding Abnormal Behavior. Arbitrary Inference is where a person draws erroneous conclusions from available evidence. They are apparently unwilling or unable to see other, more probable explanations. Eventually, this will start to take a toll on you, and eventually drain you emotionally.

On September 11 1998, I was at Surfside beach in Texas, and mother nature released her fury. On the previous night, I noticed what appeared to be crabs migrating to the sand. The winds were strong, causing the trees and vegetation to sway from side to side. I had rented a room at one of the resort homes, and at exactly 4:00 am in the morning the phone to my room rang. I couldn't imagine who would be calling, because I myself didn't even know the phone number to my room. It rang twice and stopped. I wondered who it was, so I thought I'd go and check with the owners, to see if they were the ones who had called me.

As I set my foot on the floor, I noticed there was water, and it was almost half way to my knees, just below my lower calves. During the night, tropical storm Frances had descended upon the shore. The hurricane winds were so powerful that the waves from the ocean were smashing against the wall of my room, which was on the first floor. I was worried about being electrocuted, but was able to make it outside safely. I went upstairs and awakened the owners, who were unaware of the seriousness the storm, and the damage it had already inflicted. I then asked them if they had called me a few minutes earlier, and they both said they hadn't because they were deep asleep. To this very day I'll never know who made that call, but I know that it may have saved me from drowning in my sleep.

Within hours, the emergency services issued an evacuation notice for all residents. After I paid the owners and told them I was leaving, I asked them why they weren't heeding the warning to evacuate, even though it was evident that the floodwaters were rapidly rising. They said they planned to wait it out, and if they were forced to leave, they would still come back and rebuild in the same place if their home happened to be destroyed. When I heard that, I was blown away. You'd think they would use their insurance money to build in a safer place, but they didn't take that into consideration. They still wanted to come back and rebuild in the same spot, even though it was flood prone and had caused damage worth tens of thousands of dollars to their property, and threatened their livelihoods. Ten years later on September 13, 2008, the Texas coast was hit by hurricane Ike, and this particular resort home was annihilated into oblivion.

That's the same mindset some men have. They repeatedly court the same type of women, despite their previous painful experiences with the same. There are some men who only seem to pursue and attract women who are emotionally unavailable or women with excessive emotional baggage. Even though these men have tasted the bitter sting of heartache and disappointment, for some strange reason, they gravitate toward such women. These men believe even though such a woman has the traits of their previous girlfriends, they will eventually evolve into the ideal, loving woman they desire.

It would be best to find a woman who is just as emotionally sound as you are, rather than try to rescue someone who has a lot of work to do on herself. Everybody has been disappointed at some point in life, but those who are able to manage and overcome their disappointments, are low maintenance - emotionally speaking. If you went to a car dealership, would you prefer to purchase a car with high mileage, or a car with low mileage?

I personally know guys were once very dynamic and cheerful, but ignored my advice and got involved with women who were wounded, simply because these women were attractive. Now these same cats are just as miserable as the women they are dating. Why rob yourself of your joy?

Remember the times when just waking up in the morning was something you looked forward to. Remember all the times you enjoyed your hobbies and didn't have to either ask for permission or apologize for basking in them. What happened to that person? What happened to the innocence of just enjoying your life? Who stripped you of that innocence? Where is that person now; the one who stripped you of your innocence? Does that person even value you or care for you as you did for them? That person is gone and is probably with someone else.

It's never too late to recapture your former dynamism. You just have to switch your state of mind. You can go back to being that guy filled with laughter. You start by recalling your past positive experiences and using them as a springboard to catapult you into your desired future.

Maybe you once had a dream of graduating from college, but young love caused you to marry earlier than you anticipated, and things didn't work out. You can pull yourself up to finish your education, and launch the career you always wanted. Perhaps after a failed relationship you stopped taking care of yourself and are now overweight and have health problems. Take a good look at your old photos when you were in shape. Use that memory to motivate you into losing weight and taking control of your health and eating habits. It can be done. Nothing is ever as bad as it appears. Creative imagination is now your best friend.

How about the woman you care for who suffers from a previous broken heart or emotional problems. What now? If you are whole, and have done everything you possible can in your human strength, but are still frustrated, the most you can do is say a little prayer for her. Only the divine love of God can heal a wounded heart. Move on with your life. There are frontiers out there that are waiting to be conquered, and dreams that are yet to be fulfilled by you. My high school principle always said, "Make hay, while the sun still shines. If you don't, at some point in your life you will say to yourself, I wasted time, but time does waste me now."

Chapter 4

Dealing With an Alpha Female

A man would rather be respected than be loved, because when a man is respected, he feels loved.

- Dr. Kevin Leman

During the dating process, you will discover two categories of women: The alpha female and the beta female. Alpha females tend to focus more on building relationships that revolve around their careers. They are ambitious and high achievers, and tend to define themselves by what they do for a living. Most of the friends that alpha females make are actually business associates, but they lump them in the category of friends. Alpha females refer to this as networking. Networking is the process of building business related contacts, mostly for self-serving purposes. Alpha females tend to contact their 'friends' only if they have a business transaction to carry out, or if they are working on a project together. Other than that, they'll have no use for that friend once there are no business related dealings to perform. Because alpha females tend to base a man's value on how accomplished he is, relationships with them can be very superficial. Beta females on the other hand, are ambitious and high achievers too, but place greater importance on building meaningful personal relationships rather than business contacts. Whether or not you have any business dealing with a beta female, she will value your individuality and humanity. Betas even feel comfortable wearing dresses and embrace their femininity with pride.

I have observed the kind of romantic relationships that alpha females tend to get involved in, and have noticed something rather remarkable. Alpha females are naturally drawn to alpha males because they want a man who takes charge, exudes confidence and is just as accomplished as they are. Something funny happens when an alpha female finally starts to forge a romantic relationship with an alpha male. They seem to have a very tough time separating their leadership role at the workplace from a romantic relationship outside work. Since alpha males like to take the lead in relationships, alpha females feel that by being submissive, they are stripping themselves femininity. Submission is a very dirty word to an alpha female. The result is a mental tug-of -war, and in the end, one of the two will walk away from the relationship.

I further observed that alpha females tend to build longer lasting relationships with beta males. The reason is because beta males will not challenge an alpha female on anything. They will comply with all her demands. Because he is non-threatening, an alpha female would rather be in a romantic relationship with a beta male because she knows she always has the upper hand, and her leadership role that she brings home from work, remains in tact. A lot of these relationships tend to be unfulfilling because an alpha female knows she deserves a better man, at the same time she doesn't want to lead a lonely life.

When an alpha female chooses to be unfaithful, she will seek an alpha male for the short-term, then return to her unsuspecting beta, who is more than glad just to have a woman around him. We all know highly accomplished women, who are very smart and intelligent, but end up with I-Need-To-Get-A-Life kind of guys, and shun guys who come from decent families and have a bright future ahead of them. The reason this is very common is because for most of their lives, alpha females have been the ones giving others instructions. They point out other people's weaknesses if the people they are working with are under performing in their assigned tasks.

Switching roles then becomes burdensome. When you point out to an alpha female a flaw, or try to debate her, she will become very defensive. Alpha females do not handle criticism well. They feel by being corrected, their pride is being wounded.

Alpha females like to use the phrase "I feel so insulted when you do that." The majority of the time when an alpha female starts an argument with you, she's more interested in being right than facing the truth of the matter. They have allowed their pride to cloud their judgment and rather than be respectful and demonstrate humility by admitting to an error, they unknowingly end up pushing away the alpha males they so desire. These alpha females try to rationalize their inability to keep quality men by saying that men are threatened by strong, successful, and independent women. That's actually not true. Here's the real reason why most alpha females can't keep a quality man. I read a book by Dr. Kevin Leman and he said something that's very true. He said, "A man would rather be respected than be loved, because when a man is respected, he feels loved."

The bright side of an alpha female is that she is very dependable. She calls when says she will call. In the beginning of the relationship, she will cook out of necessity, but as it progresses, she will cook for the man she desires out of the passion she has for him. Some men might be married to an alpha female, and feel that there is such a power struggle. She calls all the shots, and wants you to consult with her on everything, including giving her a detailed log of your whereabouts. Don't give up on the marriage. There is only one way you'll make an alpha female respect you. Don't use reason and logic. Don't try to get more accomplishments under your belt to impress her. If you're married to one, this is what to do. Give her the most mind-blowing experience in bed, and you'll be her king of the castle. Dominate her; she'll love you for it! Take her where no man has ever taken her before. If she's one of these wealthy women, or richissima, in the morning she will hand you all her credit cards or checkbook and ask you to take yourself on a shopping spree. Most middle class families have two vehicles. The wife always drives the luxury one, and the husband the beat-up one. This time she'll hand you the keys of her luxury vehicle, and ask you to drop her off at work, and pick her up at the end of the workday. She's gradually letting you take the lead.

However, you truly have to rock her world, for this mind shift to occur within her. Your performance has to be bravissimo! She will equate your ability to give her the most intense pleasurable moments, to potency. She will also start acting possessive toward you, and run off any other woman who tries to befriend you. Initially if she didn't have time to do chores around the house because she was too busy with her career and hired maids to do the work, she eventually will not want the maids around you, because she knows something they don't know. She'll run them off too.

Slowly by slowly she will become submissive toward you as you continue to rock on, because now you're the Mandingo. She will have a renewed respect for you, because she's now seen the light. This is strictly for married folks. If you're single, you're going to have to wait to pull this one off. After all, you don't want any female stalkers at this point in your life, do you?

Handling Beta Females

As for beta females, they tend to make the most fun and enjoyable girlfriends, and I suspect incredible wives. They take pleasure in keeping a man happy in a relationship, and don't find it burdensome to reciprocate. They are very nurturing and make the best school-teachers and nurses. Those are the two professions that women can display their natural ability to be nurturing. The reason is because in order to be effective in either one of these professions, you have to have a genuine love for people. Beta females view their professions as a calling and not just a means to sustain a living. They enjoy mingling with people regardless of whether or not they gain any-thing from the interaction, and are very easy to please. They aren't afraid to display their emotional side. Alpha males are drawn to this because naturally men want to be rescuers.

Because alpha females tend to define themselves and others by their careers and accomplishments, if you date an alpha female and let's say your company asks you to move to a different part of the country, you'll have a little problem with your woman. An alpha female will not give up her career, just to follow a man across the country. Her career defines her, so she feels that giving it up is equivalent to losing her identity. She would rather end the relation-ship with you, than move across the country or the world to be sup-portive of you.

A beta female on the other hand, will move in a heartbeat. The reason why I say that betas make the best girlfriends, and I suspect wives, is because a lot of men have careers that evolve. Companies expand and open new offices or build new franchises. Someday, they might ask you as a man, to move to the new branch and train the staff. Wouldn't you want a woman who is willing to move with you? But of course! Betas place a lot of emphasis on family and always fight to keep the family unit intact. A beta female will never withhold having sex with her husband as a way to punish or control him if she doesn't get her way. She enjoys motherhood and will even go as far as sacrificing her career just to raise her family. She feels that if she has the time, she would be doing her children an injustice by allowing a day care center to raise them, instead of her giving them her personal touch.

When you meet a group of single women, there is always an alpha female amongst them. She usually decides what events they should participate in, what restaurant they should go to, or whose car they should ride in. If you're single and looking, your greatest obstacle will be the alpha female of the clique. If you happen to befriend one of the other beta females, even though the alpha female might act friendly in your presence, she will eventually do every-thing to sabotage your relationship. She expects the other women to display their loyalty to her all the time. So if one of the women is spending a lot more time with you, than with the rest of them, the alpha female will become resentful of you no matter how friendly you are to her. You are on her turf. Since women have a special bond with each other, your beta female might feel guilty because she's known the other women longer than you, and she doesn't want to throw that away. She might end up succumbing to the persuasive voices of the other girls who are whispering into her ear.

The best way to overcome interference from an alpha female is to convince your woman to keep the relationship on the hush at the beginning stages, because that's when the relationship is most vulnerable. Once you've solidified it, then she can make the revela-tion. Girls actually can be discreet about their private lives and have the ability to keep that part of their life private, if you ask them. If you happen to date the alpha female, all the rest will find you attrac-tive and will be honored just to spend time with you. The reason is because women know that alpha females tend to set the bar high, so when she lets a man into his world, the other women will feel that he is deserving of their attention too.

On January 2 2005, I was in Stratford, England visiting a cousin. He wanted me to spend the beginning of the New Year with his family and him. After we had lunch, we started reminiscing about the good old days. I remember when he was single, he never seemed to be able to go out on dates with the women he desired. He was well spoken, well educated, and would always make a point to let women know that he wasn't in a relationship with anyone and was available. He believed by being candid, women would respond to him, but it had the opposite effect. When he would telegraph availability, women would soon lose interest in him. Eventually his brother set him up on a blind date with a great girl whom he ended up marrying.

As we were talking, he told me that all the girls that once shunned him, were now very interested in him, even though they all know that he is off the market. He couldn't understand why at some point in the past, they weren't interested in him, but now that he is married, they want him. I explained to him that when a man is in a relationship, he appears content, and is not needy for attention from other women because he gets the attention from the woman he is with. That non-neediness or being non-clingy comes across as the "I don't care or need validation from you anymore," attitude.

Women are drawn to that because they cannot believe that the man who once pursued them, isn't attracted to them anymore. They begin to have self-doubt about their abilities to attract men. The non-neediness is viewed as confidence, and a display of a strong sense of self. I explained to him further that single guys, who are successful in courting women, have women chasing them because they telegraph that same attitude. It was then that he finally was able understand the female psyche and realize there was nothing wrong with him when he was single, he just needed to be less clingy to these women by regulating the frequency he contacted them. That would create some mystique about him, and they would draw the conclusion that if he is not contacting them, he must be spending time with another woman. The inference would be that if another woman finds him worthy of her time, he is now worthy of their attention. That's why I mentioned earlier that if you start courting the alpha female, all the betas will find you desirable, and if you court a beta, not only will the other betas find you desirable, but also the alpha female will be envious of you.

Handling Nomads

Just as one of your greatest obstacles will be an alpha female, there will also be two different obstacles of the male gender – the beta male and the nomad. A nomad is a male who once was alpha, but lost his glory, and is a wandering stranger. A nomad knows a true alpha when he sees one. It is possible to be an alpha male and fall from grace. Some of the reasons alpha males lose their glory are: While he was climbing the ladder of success, he allowed arrogance to dictate his actions and alienated his allies. He eventually realized that he needed them to reach out to him, but they wouldn't.

This happens a lot in the corporate world. As men build their careers, they gain a lot of influence, power, and admiration. Everyone tends to aspire to be like them. Somehow they may lose their way and become oppressive, or forget to nurture the friends they once had because these corporate alpha males are now drunk from their own power. When that same company runs out of business and these alpha males who were sitting on top of the world now find themselves jobless, they are unable to seek help from their friends because while they were riding high, they forgot about the little guys. They didn't want to be associated with those who were less accomplished. Now they themselves have lost everything. The limo rides, expensive company dinners and vacations, and their means of generating income. So they have to start at the bottom of the ladder in order to re-build their status. Some men do and learn from humility, others aren't quite able to restore their original glory and end up becoming nomads.

Another reason an alpha male might lose his glory and become a nomad is because of bad choices. I've known men who were clinically sane, and had a bright future ahead of them, but made the wrong choice in marriage and are now divorced and struggling to pay spouse support and child support. At the end of the day, they have nothing to show for their hard work and these men end up becoming bitter about life. They resent seeing other people in happy relationships because it is a painful reminder to them of that which they lost. Their self-esteem was based on being able to support their family and enjoy a fulfilling relationship. They now have very limited supervised visitation rights to their children, and a restraining order from an angry ex-wife. It may not be an ex-wife but instead an ex-girlfriend. The loss of her could also affect some men's self-worth.

Because of that, as their self-esteem slowly erodes, so do the alpha traits they once had, and so you have a man who was once sure of himself, having to pay a psychotherapist a few hundred dollars a session, just to remind him who he is.

The third and deadliest reason an alpha male could end up becoming a nomad is plain ol' jealousy. Some men, even though they exude an aura of confidence, cannot stand to see another man succeed in life. If they've worked for decades to get where they are, and you seem to be a fast learner who is accomplishing honors at a much faster rate, you become their enemy. They seek to put you down in your absence, yet smile to your face when they are around you. Such men believe that if others notice your gifts and talents, you might steal their thunder. They never want to give credit where credit is due. Rather than use their minds to be creative, they are constantly trying to compete with you. They take your ideas, and make it seem like they are the ones who created them.

They start out as alpha males, but because, according to King Solomon, jealousy is an even more powerful emotion than anger, these men end up allowing their minds to be corrupted. Their speech loses its passion and their words sound shallow. They wind up becoming pretentious and afraid that the observer will be able to see their true character. What you have is now a nomad, who will make sure that if you as a true alpha male are trying to pursue a woman he happens to know, he will character assassinate you privately to intentionally ruin your chances, because he knows he stands no chance with that particular woman. Such a man is also very capable of committing crimes of passion. His mantra is, "If I can't have her, you can't either."

Handling Beta Males

Beta males tend to be spoilers. They see in alpha males that which they do not have, but wish to have. Unlike nomads who are openly hostile, betas try to give you the impression that they are friendly and trustworthy, and once they earn your trust, they'll violate it in a heartbeat. They will embrace you with one hand, and stab you in the back with the other.

Betas are opportunists and will not hesitate to take advantage of a woman, by sowing seeds of doubt in her mind about her alpha male boyfriend. Beta males tend to be "yes-men" to women, in anticipation of reward, because as far as personality and social skills are concerned, they are still underdeveloped. They wink and smile at you, yet in their hearts they are plotting against you. It is important for me to remind you that as you are out on the dating scene searching that special woman, these are the impediments you will face. A lot of books that pertain to relationships don't take the time to point these things out, and most books seem to bash manly men. It is my duty to correct your focus, that way you'll be well prepared when confronted with the above-described scenarios. The most important phase of any undertaking is preparation. Remember that. Let me list again who the spoilers will be while you're dating – Alpha females, nomads and beta males. These are the ones who will try to sabotage your relationships. Any time you are dating a woman and she tells you her best friend is a guy, he is either a beta male or a nomad, and will make it his mission to talk her out of the relationship.

The Alpha Male

Now that you know who the adversaries are, it's only fair that I point out who your allies will be. Contrary to what you might think, your greatest allies will be fellow alpha males, and beta females. A true alpha male knows that men have an unwritten code that you do not pursue a woman in whom another alpha is interested. They have respect for protocol. Once they find out that a woman is already spoken for, they will back off. They don't take advantage of women in their moments of vulnerability. Alpha males love and adore women and are always ready to protect them. They are not deceptive or manipulative and bring the best out of women. As for the beta females, they will defend you in your absence. They will squash any false rumors that might be intended to impugn your reputation. If they happen to be at a social gathering with your girlfriend, they will protect her from the other men who are hitting on her. You can confide in them without the fear of them using your words against you. You will eventually need an ally as you date, because there's always someone hoping that your relationship fails, or someone who's got their eye on your woman, waiting for you to slip, so they can displace you. This applies to married and non-married couples.

Counselors, psychiatrists, and psychotherapists aren't necessarily your allies. I have great respect for those professions and I know how much effort these people put into their work. The only problem I have is sometimes they focus on the symptoms of why a relationship is suffering and of course the majority of the time men tend to take the blame. The reason is because when women are having relationship problems, they tend to go to female therapists. These are women, who want to know more about men, but they are asking other women for help. If you had a tax problem, you'd go and ask an accountant to assist you, not the pool cleaner, or if you wanted to learn how to fly a plane, you'd take flying lessons from a pilot, not a bus driver. Likewise, if you want to know more about a man, ask a man, not a woman.

A woman can only tell you what works for her, and it may not necessarily work for you. A man will break it down for you, and give you a play-by-play game plan on how to get your man to respond to you, or how to fix the infringement in your current relationship. Women do not fully understand the way a man's mind works. What happens is that these women hope they'll get sympathy from a fellow woman, and are looking for someone to justify why they are miserable, rather than focus on their reality and the root cause of their misery.

All the knowledge I have acquired about women did not come from me hanging out with just men, I spent a considerable amount of time observing and researching different women and what they respond to. I am not a doctor, counselor, or therapist, nor have I ever visited one. I am simply a scientist who collects practical data based on observations of human behavior, and makes this information available to those who revere knowledge, wisdom and discernment. This book helps men become well balanced, and will also improve their outlook on life and themselves, to the point where they'll eventually inspire others. It will also help women have a better understanding of men, and what they search for in a woman.

Now that I have this vast volume of knowledge, I want to share it with the curious minds. Even if you were to go to another man and ask him to give you tips on how to succeed in the dating game, or sustain a relationship, you would still have to go out on the frontlines, and apply that knowledge to the object of your affection. You'll find out what works, and what doesn't. As you can see, women have been my greatest teachers, in pertinence to other women.

It is important that I show you how to handle both nomads and beta males.

The first assignment I gave you at the beginning of the book before seeking a meaningful relationship is to purge yourself of the negative traits that have been holding you back, and cultivate the positive ones. Once you are whole, you'll be ready to handle pretty much any scenario that comes your way as you start dating.

Since beta males and nomads come to you as friends in disguise, if you find yourself in a situation where a woman who once was receptive toward you before having a conversation with the beta male or nomad who was the spoiler, is now apprehensive in your presence, here's what to do. First, you will immediately sense that the vibes she's emitting are inconsistent with her behavior before a third party whispered in her ear. At this point, set her aside and have a sit down conversation with her. In this conversation your purpose is to define your adversary for who he really is. Use the very descriptions I have given you in this chapter and point out the reasons you are being sabotaged. You have to memorize this chapter by reading it over and over again. Once you commit it to memory, you will be able to define your adversary, whether he is the nomad or beta male, and then explain to her why they do what they do. If you have to bookmark this chapter and give it to her to read, do it.

In some instances, you have to call the spoiler out on his actions, to make him know that you are aware of his actions. You should also defend your honor when your woman inquires about what she's been hearing. Some women are naturally polite and non confrontational so they won't mention anything, but there will be a very drastic change in their behavior. They might act cold toward you, or find excuses not to do the things that you once enjoyed doing together, or reasons not to go with you to certain places. That's when you know something is wrong. A hundred percent of the time there is someone else whispering in her ear, be it male or female. It's not the time to think she's just having a bad day and whatever is bothering her will just go away, because guess what, it won't. You have to take the initiative and be proactive, by asking her why her behavior changed after coming in contact with the spoiler. Or, if the damage was done behind your back and aren't sure what her behavior is attributed to, ask her gross point blank to lay it on you. If she mentions that she's heard things, that's your opportunity to define the player haters. I earlier explained how to handle alpha females so I won't repeat myself. I am emphasizing on how to handle nomads and beta males.

What if she doesn't want to hear your side of the story and instead forms an opinion about you, and takes the side of the nomad or beta male. What do you do? In that case, dump her. She's not worthy of your time or effort. Any woman who is clinically sane and emotionally sound, will respond to truth and will be able to make an objective and informed decision regarding the direction in which the relationship will go, after listening to both sides of the story. Most women will give a man the benefit of the doubt, before drawing conclusions about him. If she feels you don't deserve the chance to explain your side, she's less interested in truth; therefore she doesn't deserve a quality man like you. Sometimes you have to be as heartless as some women are when walking away from relationships.

After you walk away from that imbalanced relationship, start dating again right away. I recommend you set up a date on the very same day you break up because that will keep you from going back to the previous relationship. Don't say anything negative about her, just act like she doesn't exist anymore. The whole point is to find a quality woman with whom you can have a quality relationship. This is the new you. The old you would be begging the woman to hear you out, and buying her expensive gifts, flowers and dinners, hoping her behavior would change and that she would respond to you positively. That old you is dead. You're a new man. Act like it.

My principles work because they have been proven and tested on the frontlines. You will not get this information from any educational institution because I am the first human being to dissect the five different elements of human behavioral patterns that are exhibited on the current dating scene. Once again these five are exhibited by: The alpha male, the beta male, the nomad, the alpha female, and the beta female.

None of this is taught in colleges, universities, conferences or seminars, because the professors, psychologists, and therapists haven't invested time to go out on the frontlines and apply these principles in person. I give you my findings from live missions and interviews I have conducted on the frontlines. These principles are sound and timeless. Even if you lived to be 300 years old, the information within this book would still be sound and applicable.

All my life, I have had a hunger for knowledge and wisdom. I have made it a point to accumulate as much of it as possible during my youth, so I can share it with others. However, I noticed that just acquiring knowledge and wisdom isn't enough to be well balanced. I watched and observed a lot of people who were wiser and more intelligent than I was, but not all of them necessarily have the ability to accurately see through situations that were obscure. They lacked a third ingredient that is necessary to make knowledge and wisdom effective. The ingredient is discernment. Discernment is being able to grasp and comprehend what is obscure, and stresses accuracy as in reading character, motives or knowing true friends. Police officers and people who work in the criminal justice system are trained to apply this particular ingredient in their profession. Another word for discernment is insight, which again is the power or act of seeing through a situation.

Once I made this discovery, I made it my objective to cultivate discernment. Unlike wisdom and knowledge that can be acquired at weekend seminar or through intensive study, discernment has to be cultivated. You have to be exposed to as many different scenarios as possible, in order to apply it accurately and effectively.

I have made things easy for you. You won't have to conduct all the research or studies that I did. I am giving all three ingredients – knowledge, wisdom and discernment, in this book. I will transfer them upon you through what I refer to as impartation. At the end of the book, you will have a sound decision making process when it comes to relationships and human behavior. The tools in this book are applicable to all areas of life. In the marketplace, these tools will help you discern good business partners, and the right ventures to undertake. In the sports arena, you'll be able accurately read into situations that come before you, because you are now a student of human behavior. In religious settings you'll have insight into the character of those in high places and will enable you to make a sound judgment as to whether you want to be under their leadership or not. In the corporate world, you'll be able to discern people's motives, strengths, and value, and will be able to hire competent and quality employees. Of course in relationships, you'll be able to discern someone of quality who deserves your pursuit or the one who is simply wasting your time.

Chapter 5

Cultural Differences Among Women

Imprinted on every man's DNA is a code that states, "A man will always gravitate and bond to a woman who makes him feel worthwhile because that's how men are genetically calibrated."

-*e*Nigma

During your courtship, you will discover that you cannot approach women from different cultures in the same way as women from your culture, and be successful with them. You might get an Asian woman to respond to you when you approach her a certain way, but that method may not work with a white or black woman. It is for this very reason that I have included a chapter to address this, because I want you to be a well balanced, quality man. There are several books written by so-called love gurus or experts, telling you that their principles or methods can help you attract any woman. None of those books talk about the specific cultural differences I am about to mention; they lump all women into one category. They do not consider an important fact that women from different cultures or ethnicities have different temperaments and belief systems.

In foreign cultures and countries, when a woman informs her parents that she is dating a man, the very first question they ask her is, "Whose son is he?" In America it is different. The parents ask, "What does he do?" In America it seems that the measure of someone is based on what that person does. That's the reason why when people in America are at a social gathering and are being introduced to each other, the person doing the introduction says, "This is so and so, he does such and such, or he works for such and such a company." Nobody is concerned about who your parents are. They could be drug dealers or bank robbers but if you have a decent job, and are making an honest living, nobody will care about your parents.

That's not the case when handling women from foreign cultures. The girl's parents want to know who and how you were raised. I don't care if you are in a respectable profession, if your parents are not honorable people, the girl's parents will forbid her to continue the relationship with you. I'll explain why.

In most of these cultures, people believe that the values and morals of the parents are passed on to the children. It's the same 'monkey see, monkey do' principle. In other words if you have renegade parents, it is believed that they will instill those same principles in the children. So a girl's father knows that you will eventually have kids with his daughter, but since your values and basic convictions are compromised, they believe your children will turn out like you. They do not want to take that chance, so they will come between your relationship with their daughter.

If on the other hand, if you have honorable parents, no matter how much trouble you get yourself into, the girl's parents will give you a pass and the benefit of the doubt. They believe you eventually will turn out to be as honorable as your parents. In essence in foreign cultures, they would prefer their children to marry into reputable families, whereas in America parents would prefer their children to marry those with reputable jobs or careers. The infinite (your inner man – who you are), in foreign cultures is more valued than the temporal (what you do.)

In foreign cultures you can have a conversation with a girl's parents, and not once will they ask you what you do, they'll just dig for information about your upbringing. In America it is impossible to have a conversation with a girl's parents without them asking you what you do for a living that same day you are introduced to them. It is very common for people who come from unknown families to rise to the top of their profession in America, and get special treatment because of what they do or the company they work for. On the contrary, if you are from a reputable family in a foreign culture, you will get special treatment, even long after the parents are deceased. If you go to a bank and the line is long, but you come from an honorable family, the teller will blatantly tell you to come to the front of the line, that way you won't have to wait. In hospitals, you'll never have to sit in the waiting area even though you came late and there were a dozen people who arrived before you. What's surprising is that the people who were there before you, won't complain because they feel if you have high status, you deserve to be treated that way. The family name carries a lot of weight.

Most people wonder why Asian kids excel in class; that's because their families put a very high premium on education. To get low grades in the Asian culture is to dishonor the family name, so they are raised from childhood, to uphold the family's legacy. When dating, they want their daughters to go out with someone whose family takes education as seriously as they do.

I would like to tackle the four dominant cultures in America, and how to handle the women from these cultures. The four different kinds of women you will encounter are Hispanic, Black, White and Asian women. All four should be approached differently.

One thing you have to know is, no matter how good and effective your approach is, there are some women who will reject you, not because they don't find you desirable, but because they want to honor their parents' wishes. For instance, if a very wealthy man has only two daughters and he comes from the old school, he might drop a hint at them that he wants them to marry within their race, and if they don't, he will exclude them from his will. In cases like that, a woman isn't going to tell you that there is a fortune at stake, she'll just blow you off no matter how tight your game is. The same could happen to a son who is indirectly forced to relinquish a relationship that is outside his race if he wishes to inherit the multi-million dollar family business. These are issues that none of the love gurus talk about, but are valid and happen everyday.

It may not even be a cultural issue. You might come from the same culture or race, but the parents may feel uncomfortable with you, because you can't hold a job and they are concerned about whether you'll be able to support their daughter or not. Because she wants to honor her parents, she might let you off gently, while complimenting you on how great a guy you are, and how lucky the woman will be who will marry you. The same could happen with a guy. If the woman he is dating has a questionable reputation or associations, even though they both belong to the same race, the guy's parents, especially the mother, will convince the son to drop her like a bad habit. Mothers want daughters-in-law that they can be proud of. A guy will normally let her off gently by not returning her calls, or he will always be busy, until the relationship finally diminishes. His excuse will usually be, "We just grew apart." So don't take anything personally and think your approach was ineffective; it might have been effective, but there simply may be some other dynamics that are coming into play.

On October 15, 2005 when I was in Venice Italy, I found out first hand how important it was to be able to distinguish different cultures from different regions of the country. Among the most fascinating experiences in Venice, are the gondola rides around the Grand Canal. It is important for you to understand the Venetians before taking a ride. For instance, initially your guide might charge you 12 Euros for the entire ride. However, at the end of the ride, he may end up asking you for 16 Euros. If you ask how it happened, he might say, "The ride was 12 Euros, but I also sang for you, which is an extra four Euros." So before you take a ride on the gondola, you have to make it clear even before you get into the boat. No singing. No playing musical instruments. Just the ride. The same applies to dating women from different cultural backgrounds. It is important that you understand their background, communication process and upbringing. I am here to help you solve that.

Chapter 6

Courting Asian Women

Asian women are perhaps the most submissive and somber women you'll ever meet. In the Asian culture, it is often considered a sign of defiance to look people in the eye. They'll interpret that as you wanting to challenge the other person into a confrontation. So if you happen to meet an Asian woman who isn't giving you much eye contact, don't stress. It's just her upbringing. Asians rarely raise their voices and tend to keep their opinions to themselves. As a matter of fact, throughout your lifetime, you may never hear an Asian, male or female, using a cuss word. They consider that to be beneath their dignity.

I have always tried to decode a phenomenon I see happening very often. I've noticed that white men have a fascination for Asian women. When I first discovered this, I could never seem to understand why it was so. Every time I saw an attractive petite Asian woman, there was usually a white guy at her side. I thought it was perhaps a coincidence, but throughout my travels, even to distant lands, it's the same story. A white man will most likely pick an Asian woman over the most beautiful white woman, if the opportunity presented itself. White women understand this reality very well. That's why if you're in a classroom or at your workplace, or social gathering with quite a few Asian or foreign women, white women will not play hard to get with you. They know that American men have such a fascination for foreign women, who are actually their biggest competition.

I thought I would study Asian men to see how they responded to women. I discovered something interesting. Most of the Asian men I observed, were drawn to or courting white women. So here we have white men going nuts over Asian women, and Asian men going crazy over white women. As a behavioral scientist, I decided it was time to put my brainpower to work in order to come up with an explanation to my findings.

According to the U.S Census Bureau, whites are currently the majority race. It therefore makes sense in terms of proportionality that most white men are in positions of power or influence. During their busy workdays, they have to manage companies, supervise workforces, build teams and train employees. This role that they assume in the workplace is something they want to separate themselves from while they are not working. In order for one to do that, one has to find a partner who is non-confrontational and laid back. That's where Asian women come in to play. So more and more, white men find themselves gravitating toward Asians, not so much because of their physical attributes, but because they find that these Asian women complement their personalities.

When approaching Asian women, you have to be gentle. Don't speak in a loud voice. Calibrate the volume of your voice to match theirs. If you have a crude vocabulary, you'll be doing yourself a disservice to use it in their presence. Don't rush into the relationship or start complimenting them on their physical features. They might get the impression, that you are only interested in their exotic look. Instead, talk about things that stimulate their intellect. Subjects that involve functionality are best suited for Asians. Examples of such topics include: Information Technology, Telecommunications, manufacturing, or topics that involve practical undertakings. You only use these topics as icebreakers. Once you begin to engage them in a conversation, switch to family oriented material, because topics regarding functionality aren't really romantic nor do they have depth. You simply use them to stimulate their intellect, after that, start talking about things of substance. Avoid physical contact but remain in close proximity with the woman. Asians traditionally bow as a form of greeting. There is minimal body contact. Because they are not used to that kind of contact, as a stranger, allow her to invite you into her world. If she likes you, she will find an excuse to initiate physical contact with you. Once you gain her trust, she will do anything you request her to do.

Asian women perhaps are the only women who do not flake. They, together with women from Eastern Europe, are very comfortable in embracing their femininity. If you make an appointment to meet an Asian woman at a certain time, she'll show up. When she says she'll call, she calls. When her phone rings, she answers. This is something all men find irresistible, because the majority of women will flake on you even after giving you their word.

Asian women almost never break dates. Honor is a very important factor that enables them to define who they are. Because of their pursuit for excellence, their submissive nature, and feeling comfortable in letting men take the lead, white men tend to gravitate toward Asians. This is not to say that their white, black, or Hispanic female counterparts do not have or value the qualities I have mentioned. They do, but Asian women are more likely to exude all these qualities, all the time.

My role as a scientist allows me to document my observations, but because I am also a trained journalist, I have to present both sides of the coin to create a fair analysis.

The downside of women in the Asian culture is that they tend to be passive. The danger in passivity is that they are likely to be taken advantage of, which might lead to abuse in the relationship. The lack of assertiveness might be looked upon as a weakness, and since Asians tend to be non-confrontational, they are likely to keep any conflict, whether internal or external to themselves and not seek help.

Over all, I suspect they make incredible and loyal wives or girlfriends, and can motivate any man who has mediocre ambitions, to want to excel in life. Also because they are very feminine, men naturally are forced to get in touch with their sensitive side as a way of reciprocation. The result can be a fulfilling and well-balanced relationship between two people from different cultures.

Chapter 7

Courting White Women

White women, according to my findings, are the most uninhibited women on earth. No other segment of women is as proactive as white women. They get things done. They have a sense exploration that is unmatched, and are also the most candid women you'll ever meet. You can meet a white woman and within forty-five minutes, she'll have told you her entire life story. I believe they do that because they want to know from the get go that you will accept them for whom they are. If you show any apprehension because of something a white woman said, she will immediately build a brick wall that you may never be able to penetrate. As far as their sense of exploration is concerned, I have conducted interviews with them, and the majority would be willing to travel to a remote village or area of the earth, just for the sake of exploration. You'll be very surprised if you ever get a chance to go on an African Safari that the majority of the people traveling will be white.

Even though white women are direct and candid, you shouldn't approach them in the same manner. You might be successful in getting a phone number or even going on the first date, but later you might not hear from them again, if you rush things. Since they like to explore, this is your opportunity to let them explore you for who you are. How do you do that? Give them small bits of information about yourself at a time. Just because she told you her entire life story, doesn't mean she'll respond to you if you do the same. Stretch out the information and give it to her over a spread out period of time. This makes her wonder and want to even explore you more. The reward is in the exploration. The more questions she asks herself, the more she becomes interested in you. Eye contact is very important to indicate that you are focused on her. You can then apply the techniques I listed in the chapter one that deal with the approach, to completely win her over.

A lot of the quality white women you'll meet, will already have established careers, so if you're not as accomplished as they are, don't make up lies about yourself. Because the white population is large, they have a bigger pool from which to choose their men. They therefore won't have a problem leaving you for someone else if they discover that the relationship was built on falsehoods.

Something white women find attractive is a man with ambition, even though he may be struggling in life to make ends meet. All you have to exhibit is a passion for achieving your dreams. Most women of other ethnic groups will commend and even acknowledge your efforts but won't want to be in a relationship with you if you have a lower status than they. The reason why ambition builds desire in white women is because they know that if you are passionate and driven to succeed in achieving your life goals, once you apply that same kind of drive and passion to the relationship, it too will eventually be rewarding and fruitful. They are looking at the bigger picture and are not concerned about the here and now.

Because they are uninhibited, they tend to fall in love a lot quicker than their counterparts. They are not afraid to allow themselves to feel vulnerable. That's where they get the thrill. If you want to have a fulfilling relationship, you are going to have to be objective to a white woman's suggestions and desires. If she suggests something and you act shocked, she will become very apprehensive and reserved, and to a small extent withdrawn thereafter. From then on, the relationship will start going downhill and I guarantee you she will find someone else who is willing to explore and be adventurous with her. When she's in love with you, she'll give you latitude on almost anything. She'll always be understanding, as long as you give her attention. That's all white women want from a romantic relationship – your attention.

I also have to tell you about the other side of white women. Because most of the quality women will already have their careers, if you're a man of quality too, your biggest problem will be the power struggle. A white woman will get away with whatever you allow her to get away with. The more you allow her to get away with, the more power she attains in the relationship. As a man, if you lose your power, she equates that with you losing your manhood, and her desire to want to be with you will plummet. She doesn't want to have a man she can walk all over.

Please understand that when I use the word power, I mean influence in the relationship. Out of frustration, because you'll be struggling to reclaim your lost power, you might end up losing your focus on her. One of the greatest insults you can ever commit against a white woman is to neglect her and not give her the attention she feels she deserves in the relationship. A white woman will even forgive you, if you cheat on her, but one thing she will never overlook if the two of you are in a relationship is neglect. I know a lot of women of other ethnicities who are happy as long as their man maintains the household or takes care of them, even though he is always gone, and is seldom at home. White women are different. Expensive jewelry, clothing, cars or lifestyle are meaningless to them if they feel they don't have your attention. When their love grows cold, it's almost impossible to reverse it to its previous state. That is one of the biggest problems you'll encounter with white women.

The result is obvious and in most cases, such relationships may not even be salvageable. The sting of being ignored and neglected by you will always get into the way of any reconciliation happening.

The reason why it is easier for a white woman to forgive a man who has been unfaithful to her, than one who neglects her is simple. My research shows that as long as she is convinced that you cheated out of moments of weakness, she will also believe that you weren't emotionally attached to the other woman. She will feel that your emotional affection still belongs to her. Neglecting her, breaks the emotional bond that holds your relationship, and once that emotional bond no longer exists, the immediate feeling she experiences is betrayal. It is the emotional wound caused by betrayal that could derail a once solid relationship. That's when arguments start, as a by-product of resentment.

On a brighter note, white women tend to be willing to take the blame for their share of mistakes, rather than point fingers. Admitting one's role in creating conflict is the first step to resolving it quickly. It is my belief that once the channels are open with a free flow of communication, the minor misunderstandings can be contained to avoid a major conflict. My advice to you if you want to be successful in courting white women, is to follow a simple business principle invented by Dr. Larry Ruddell. The principle is, 'Major in the Minors.'

Chapter 8

Courting Hispanic Women

Of all the women I have encountered, Hispanic women tend to be the most passionate ones. They are also the most family oriented women I know. Hispanic women are experts at stroking a man's ego to make him feel like a king. They take their relationships very seriously and will even go as far as sacrificing their careers, just to spend time with or support their families. Hispanic women are straightforward if they are interested in you. You won't have to second-guess their intentions or motives, because they use a direct approach. They will not hesitate to pursue a man they are interested in or find a way of getting his attention. Most of their activities revolve around their families and communities. You therefore should approach Hispanic women with the understanding that there will be moments when they specifically have to make time to be with their relatives, and won't always accommodate your needs.

Once you have this understanding in mind, you will not feel as though you aren't being taken seriously if a Hispanic woman has to end a date early to tend to family obligations. The quickest way to break ice after approaching a Hispanic woman is to talk about cultural themes like travel, music, and the performing arts. With the exception of blacks, I haven't met a race of people that enjoys dance as much as Hispanics. Even the older and mature ones love a good Latin rhythm. An ideal date would include asking her to go out dancing with you. Practice your Latin moves and you will make a great impression. If you have two left feet, all you have to do is spin her around, every now and then. As long as she's moving her body, she'll be happy.

You also have to exhibit a certain level of cultural depth. Their culture is woven deep into the very essence of who they are. Show the willingness to learn about their culture, because by doing that, you are showing that you not only take her seriously, but also are willing to mingle with her culture. If you come across as standoffish, she'll be turned off. Once again, after you've built rapport and she feels comfortable with you, you may follow the principles in chapter one to tie all the loose ends.

Hispanic women also tend to be very superstitious. Since the majority of them have a high affinity for religion, they tend to incorporate their beliefs into their daily life, but aren't necessarily dictated by those beliefs.

Let's take a look at the other side of Hispanic women. Because they are very passionate in their love lives, they are also passionate in their wrath. Hispanic women will pick on you just to see how much you can endure. Just when you think the relationship is flowing freely and peaceful, they'll create drama at an unexpected moment. You can act laid back with Asian women and never experience conflict, that's not the same with Hispanic women. Because they are aggressive, they assume you too will have the same level of aggression to match theirs. The result will be one heck of a ride that you won't soon forget.

You don't talk things out with Hispanic women because you'll never win. You simply walk away, or if you're married to one, go to another room and lock the door behind you until the dust settles. If you leave the door open, she'll follow you around and the drama will never end. Even the petite Hispanic women will challenge you despite your physical size or strength. If you resist their challenges and ignore them, they'll start talking smack to you, in hopes of getting you to react. Because the law is always on the women's side, follow my advice and just walk away.

What really sets off Hispanic women to become so passionate in their wrath? I believe that they ignore all the little errors you make or wrong things you say during the course of the relationship. Because they are very supportive of their men, they won't mention the offense at the time it happens. They'll simply shrug it off, unlike black or white women who will 'check you' immediately after the offense occurs. In the meantime, you as the guy, will continue to make the little mistakes because you assume just because she hasn't said anything, the relationship is flawless. After she's had enough and can't take it anymore, you'll experience her fury that accumulated with time.

The good thing is once the conflicting situation subsides, she will reward you because she knows you are still her man. She won't apologize to you though. However, she will never withhold her affection from you or play mind games. When you are courting a Hispanic woman, she's not looking at you as just a boyfriend, she sees you as a lifetime mate. Hispanic women are raised to stand by their men. They do not believe in divorce, unless violence is involved and their safety is in danger, or in cases of abandonment, which might occur after being duped into a marriage of convenience. Other than those two circumstances, Hispanic women take their sacred vows very seriously, and pass on their way of thinking to their offspring.

Chapter 9

Courting Black Women

Black women are by far the most resilient women in the world. They are also the most poetic and spiritual women you'll ever meet. They are naturally very endearing and tend to use terms such as honey, baby, or sweetie, even when communicating to strangers. Since they are very matriarchal, they tend to display that side of themselves through words of endearment. Black women tend to initiate body contact as a way to create emphasis, or acknowledge a point. So don't mistake her touch or words of endearment for interest in you. Those generic signs should not be taken seriously if you are looking for a green light.

After you approach a black woman, you absolutely have to gain her trust. Even before you make the approach, a black woman will assume you intend to hit on her. All her defenses will be up by the time you make the approach. If your approach is tight, you will always get the phone number. The first date will determine how long you will last. You have to make a very good impression in order to keep a black woman's interest. They value manliness and inner strength as well as accomplishments. You'll have a very tough time finding a quality black woman if you have nothing productive happening in your life. Confidence is also a must. Any hesitation on your behalf in asking for the phone number is viewed as weakness.

Dating black women can be tricky. You see black women come in different packages that I'll describe to you. You have the black women that were born and raised in America, but you also have black women from the U.K, Africa, and the Caribbean. There is a very big difference between black Americans, and foreign black women. Black women from the Caribbean, Africa, or the U.K, tend to put a great deal of emphasis on how educated a man is. You have to absolutely be well educated if you expect to have a fulfilling relationship with them. A lot of foreign black women have roots in third world countries, so they believe that if they were able to rise to the top based on the education they acquired, it's inexcusable for a man not to be able do the same. Another factor I discovered as to why they are drawn to educated men has to do with genetics. They simply want to have smart kids. They know that if both parents are intelligent, there is a high likelihood that their children will be intelligent and value education too.

I stumbled across this discovery by mistake when I first conducted my research on foreign black women. They seemed to be very interested in knowing the level of education the man had, or his academic achievements. I asked why they focused on that, but they just told me, they wanted to feel secure that the men had the ability to be good providers. Education facilitates that. It was after I did in depth research that the word 'children' kept popping up. When I dug further, all admitted that they also wanted to have intelligent children. They only admitted after I pressed them. After that, I was able to conduct full-blown studies to verify my conclusion. The higher your I.Q, the more respected and desirable you become to foreign black women. As far as looks go, they like men who are stylish, or sharp dressers. They also believe that even if a man isn't that physically attractive, but is intelligent, in shape and understands fashion, it will make up for his deficiencies in the looks department.

Black women in America are different. If you are not well educated but have potential, are a great provider, and romantic, they will consider you. They don't put much emphasis on how intelligent the offspring will turn out to be. The most important thing a black American woman wants from her man is to be valued and celebrated for whom she is.

When a black woman falls in love with you, one of the most common ways her love is manifested is through her cooking. Another thing I observed is that when she cooks for you, she wants you to eat the meal right there and then. She wants to know that you enjoy the meal and her cooking was not in vain. With women of other ethnicities, you can get away with saying; "I'll just wrap it up and eat it at my place." That wouldn't work with black women.

One of the greatest insults you can ever commit against a black woman is to refuse a meal she has cooked for you. She'll take it very personally because in her eyes, rejecting her cooking is equivalent to rejecting her. In December 2004, I was visiting one of my sisters, and she decided to cook for me breakfast. Part of the breakfast included scrambled eggs surrounded by sliced tomatoes. I ate everything except the tomatoes. After I was done, I took my plate to her kitchen, and she looked at the plate with the leftover tomatoes but didn't say a word. She has never cooked anything for me again.

In the relationships I've had with black women, if one makes me a home cooked meal, I now make it a point to remind them how delicious it was. You'll be surprised how willing they'll be to cook for you on a regular basis if you show an appreciation for their cooking.

I have to talk about the beauty salon. Nothing can come between a black woman and an appointment she has with her beautician. If you schedule a date on the day she has to get her hair or nails done, it'll have to happen after her appointment. I have never met a black woman who was willing to cancel an appointment at the beauty salon for anything.

Regarding kissing a black woman, never ask a black woman if you should kiss her. After you've built rapport, this is exactly what you should do and say. You lean in slowly and say these exact words: "Give Daddy some sugar." You then go for the kiss. It is very important that you first make her feel at ease with you, or else you might get smacked right across your face. The reason why you should never ask a black woman whether you should kiss her is because by asking her, you are displaying self-doubt. You're telling her that you are not sure if it is okay. In her mind, she will get turned off by your lack of confidence, and will obviously object.

Since black women want a man who is secure and displays inner strength, if you are thinking of courting a one, you need to improve your inner game. By saying, "Give Daddy some sugar," two things happen to her psychologically. First, you are causing her to be proactive by using the active verb 'give.' Secondly, you are taking the lead while being sweet at the same time when you say, 'Daddy some sugar.' The combination of making her proactive, and displaying confidence while being gentilissimo is something black women find irresistible.

One summer I had just finished my workout at a local gym and received a phone call from a woman I was seeing. She wanted me to go to her place and pick up a meal she baked for me. I was wearing a bandana, with loose fitting clothes, but I decided to just go straight to her place without changing, because I knew the visit would be brief. When I arrived and she saw me, she was unusually excited, and didn't want me to leave. I told her I had to go run some errands. Out of curiosity, I asked her why she was delirious. She gave me a naughty look and said, "Every once in a while I want you to dress like a thug. I like that thug look the bandana gives you." I couldn't believe what I was hearing! This was a very classy woman, who wore nothing but designer business suits to work and pumps. Her hair was always meticulously done, and her English was perfect and impeccable. Despite all that, she responded positively to the thug persona. This was a revelation I had once again stumbled across by accident.

You see every black American woman secretly would want to get some good thug loving. Even the nice and dignified ladies have the same wish. They just don't talk about it. If you ever meet a black American woman who says it's not true, she's lying to you. I can say with absolute steadfastness, that the accuracy of my findings is irrefutable. They are not looking for a thug in the real sense, they just want you to unleash the animal within you every once in a while.

I also have to mention something about white women in relation to blacks. Several white women of all ages have confided in me that the majority of white women have a secret desire to be intimate with black men. It is called The Forbidden Fruit Syndrome. This is something that white women keep on the hush-hush, because they would rather avoid being in conflict with black women, or face their wrath and hostility, as a result of action taken on behalf of white women.

To be fair to other ethnic groups, I also have to mention the other side of black women. One of the biggest problems you'll face when dating black women is that they always feel the need to get the approval of their friends, regarding the men they are dating. Anytime a black woman you've only been courting briefly mentions that she wants you to meet her friends, it's a set up. She wants them to screen you for her, so they can compare notes.

One Sunday afternoon, a lady I was seeing told me she wanted to go cruising with me because she enjoyed my company. I jumped into my vehicle, drove to her house and picked her up. As we were cruising around, she told me she had to stop at a particular venue to drop off something. When we got to the place, she insisted that I walk in with her. Guess what . . . somehow eight of her friends happened to swing by a few minutes before we arrived. Now what are the chances of that happening? But hey, coincidences do happen. She introduces me to them, and all of a sudden, all nine women happened to feel like taking a leak at the same time. I told them I'd wait for them, and they all headed for the ladies restroom. Do you really think that was another coincidence? You know they weren't taking leaks; they were in there comparing notes regarding me.

The problem is, no matter how nice you are to all her friends, there is always one of them who won't like you. She's also usually the least attractive one, or the one that's out of shape. She's the one who will always try to talk her out of the relationship and come between you. So right there, you have an uphill battle. Another thing my studies have revealed about black women is that the ones that are attractive and educated, feel the need to make guys go through hoops. You can't even just talk to an attractive black woman without her thinking you are trying to get into her pants, so she'll give you an attitude even when you just say, "Hello." Not all guys are trying to bone you. Black women need to relax.

What's interesting is that even when you approach those single pretty black women, they'll act like they have a boyfriend, even though they don't. This boyfriend is somehow invisible because you never see them together, yet the women try to convince you that he exists. They are always running around with their less attractive girlfriend though, not the boyfriend. He's invisible. Maybe he's too busy. Who knows? They'll even go as far as wearing a fake ring, to make-believe they are spoken for. You know who they are. Their pride will not let them admit that they are attractive but still single, and have no man, so they make up the "I have a boyfriend" story, as a way to stroke their own egos. When you finally get them to go out with you, they'll act like they are doing you a favor, because they just dumped the invisible boyfriend in order to be with you.

Sadly what happens is a lot of these pretty black women who make men go through hoops or act hostile toward them, find themselves still single in their late thirties and even forties. This is because somebody lied to them that the perfect man would show up someday. Amazingly, they believe that myth. These are the same women who go around asking themselves, "Where have all the good men gone?" If they weren't so self-absorbed, they'd open their eyes and realize that good men are everywhere, waiting to be recognized. Black women do themselves a great disservice and have nobody but themselves to blame, when they portray that kind of persona. It reinforces the belief of mainstream society that black women are angry, even though that may not necessarily be true. It also drives away their potential mates.

On April 6, 2007, Oprah Winfrey did a show in which she quoted statistics that showed that 70 percent of black women are single. Her statistics reinforce what I am talking about in this chapter. If you are also observant, you'll notice that in most social gatherings, or houses of worship, most of the pretty black women are single, which is consistent with Oprah's stats. Now, if you have an issue with those numbers and you are a single black woman who happened to stumble across this book, don't take it out on me; those are Oprah's numbers, not mine. At the end of this book, there is a section called 'Notes' in which I include a link to a YouTube video of this particular show. You will also find other useful references and supporting material regarding the facts I lay out throughout this entire book.

Most beautiful women who are single have a chip on their shoulder. A lot of the beautiful single black women have a chip on both shoulders. A simple change in attitude is enough to land these women the men they've been looking for. Remember, all the unattractive women who talked them out of their relationships are likely to be happily married by this time and are raising families of their own. Eventually, these pretty black and single women get to a certain point in life and realize their biological clocks are ticking. Out of loneliness or perhaps the human need for companionship, they end up settling for someone they would never have given a second look while they were still in their twenties and biologically sound.

Men in a sense have it made more than women. The older a man gets, the higher he becomes in status. This is because when men are younger in their twenties or thirties, they are still trying to establish themselves. Once they hit their forties and fifties, they pretty much have built a nest egg and are financially secure. This sense of security produces confidence and poise, which women find attractive. These men who once had problems attaining women when they were younger, now have power and influence. These ingredients enable them to attract even women half their age. Most of those men tend to pursue much younger women as a means of revalidating their potency.

How do you overcome a pretty black woman who wants you to go through hoops? The quickest way to overcome that problem is by dating women of other races who are just as attractive, or even more attractive than they are. That seems to be the only way that the pretty black women will take you seriously. They know the reality they live in, and how hard it is to find the right man. Just because a woman from a certain race is attractive, that does not nullify the attractiveness of a woman from a different race. When they see you with a much prettier woman of a different race, they are humbled because they now realize that you've got options.

One thing all women should realize is that, imprinted on every man's DNA is a code that states, "A man will always gravitate and bond to a woman who makes him feel worthwhile because that's how men are genetically calibrated. Even though men are visual beings, it's not always about eye-candy. A clinically sane man will pick an average looking woman with the right attitude and a great personality, over an attractive one with a nasty attitude and no personality.

However, if you find a quality black woman who values your worth, treat her with dignity, and she'll devote herself to you. The wonderful thing about black women is that once they fall in love with you, they'll defend your honor in an almost militant way. If you show them how much you treasure them, they will surrender to you in unimaginable ways. You will become their confidant and they will invest themselves in the relationship so utterly. Perhaps the most positive thing about black women is that they have an incredibly strong work ethic. It's no wonder that the majority of quality black women I know out-earn their black male counterparts.

Chapter 10

Dating on College Campuses

Dating Younger Women (18-24 years)

Dating on a college campus is like living in a little town.

Word gets around.

- *e*Nigma

If you're in college and are thinking of getting involved in a relationship with a woman, you have to be very cautious. The college scene is a whole different ball game than the real world. College age women are usually between 18 to 24 years of age, and that is the demographic that flakes the most. In college, women are still trying to find themselves. I was very surprised that there were some women I knew, who didn't even know what they wanted to do with their lives on the day they graduated. I would strongly advise against forming any serious relationships with these younger women. You also have to guard your reputation because one small misunderstand regarding your intentions, could cause you to be labeled negatively.

The people who need to be very cautious are the athletes, or those on scholarships. Usually at fraternity parties, a lot of things can happen. Women at these parties are very uninhibited and permissive; you don't even have to have game if you're a guy. That's the women's chance to release their naughty side. A lot of alcohol is involved and when people get zonked, anything can happen between you and the woman you are with. When the woman is finally in her right mind and reflects on her actions, she might feel a deep sense of guilt, depending on what happened between the two of you. The result of that guilt might trigger buyer's remorse within her. No woman ever wants to feel like a 'nafka.' Even though your actions might have been consensual, your image and reputation will be at her mercy. You better pray that you never have a falling out with her because she could accuse you of anything, and it will be her word against yours. Dating on a college campus is like living in a little town. Word gets around. Even though nothing may have happened between you and her, if you were in the vicinity, you could become guilty by virtue of your presence. Just ask the athletes at Duke Lacrosse University what happened to them. So tread softly if you're still in college. These are conversations parents should have with their sons, before sending them off to college. But hey, our parents grew up in a different time, when the dynamics weren't the same as we have today, so you can't blame them. Since I am a very observant cat, I'm passing my research and findings on to you, to keep you from getting in trouble, just like I was able to stay out of trouble but still have fun. Think of me as your big brother pointing you in the right direction and you'll be just fine. Does this mean you cannot date in college? No, that's not what I am saying. In fact I know a lot of people who married their college sweethearts. I'm just saying do it with caution. If you're fortunate, you might even find a woman whose level of maturity exceeds that of her age mates.

The reason why I would not recommend you having a serious relationship with the younger crowd is because that demographic tends to be unstable, easily distracted, and in most cases undependable. They haven't felt the bitter sting of what it's like to live in the real world where they have no safety net. If you want to verify what I am saying, just ask any college professor what the most irritating habit they have to deal with in class is. They will unanimously tell you, it's students text-messaging or playing with their laptops in the middle of lectures. I've witnessed it myself. What's funny is that the guys almost never exhibit that kind of behavior.

You can have a relationship in college, but don't get too serious. People who do not take my advice and start dating these 18 to 24 year olds seriously, find out that they don't answer their phones, reply their e-mails, or return phone calls. So these men come back to me and tell me I was right, but by then they are already worn out emotionally.

The remedy is to date women outside your college campus if you're looking for a relationship with depth. You have to import. The term import in this context refers to befriending a woman from outside your college circles, who provides you with companionship. When you're taking walks on campus, nobody knows whom she is. At social functions, she's your date. You should have an active life outside of college anyway. Pick up the Sunday newspaper and check the entertainment section for social events taking place. Be on top of your game and up-to-date on the fun things happening around town. Don't just make friends with your classmates; make friends out there in the real world. When you graduate, your classmates will move to different cities in search for careers, and you'll have to build new relationships all over again. You might as well build those connections while you're still in school. Be social. Don't be a hermit.

When you date outside your campus, I would recommend you date an older woman. If you're in your early twenties, find someone who is in her mid to late twenties. Those women tend have a stronger sense of self, because they have outgrown the college phase. They know what it's like to roll up their sleeves and make things happen. They are a lot wiser than the younger women, and will help you remain focused on your goals. They don't pretend to be talking on their cell phones just to give you the impression that they might be important. These women actually will pickup the phone when you call them; and if you find one who already has her own pad, your classmates will never see you on the weekends. Now once you are in your mid to late twenties, you can then switch back to younger women, or women your age. Just try to make sure they are not younger than twenty-four years of age.

The positive aspect about dating younger women between the ages of 18 to 24 is that when they fall for you, they fall really hard. When these younger women are in love, they are stubbornly in love. Nobody, I mean nobody, can ever talk them out of the relationship. Not even their parents. These women are willing do anything to prove their love for you. They are unwavering and resolute. The love that comes from them is so pure. They have very minimal baggage or emotional scars, and chances are, you might even be their first serious boyfriend. These younger women will even change schools, just to be close to you. Their minds haven't been corrupted by the daily grind. They are very easy to please and extremely low maintenance. They are unafraid of change and easily adapt to new situations.

In the June 2005 edition of GQ magazine, they featured an interview with five American soldiers from the Pennsylvania National Guard, who guarded the former Iraqi dictator Saddam Hussein for almost 300 days. These soldiers told GQ that during that time, they were able have some interesting conversations with Saddam. They said among the topics that came up, was the subject about women. As I continued to read the article, I realized that even a dictator like Saddam, knew a thing or two about women. His advice to these five young soldiers about women was, "You gotta find a good woman. Not too old, not too young. Not too smart, not too stupid. In the middle." The old man had figured it out.

Chapter 11

Courting Older Women

Before I go into detail about older women, I have to issue a stern warning to you about them. They can be very addictive. When you start dating older women, the greatest challenge you'll face is reverting to younger women. Older women are in a class of their own. Older women and younger women are as different as night and day. In a lot of aspects, younger women cannot touch older women. When it comes to self-image, older women have a stronger sense of self, and are comfortable in their own skins. When it comes to stability, they already have established careers and are financially independent. When it comes to experience ...forget about it! They'll turn your out.

On August 20 1992, I made a trip to Moscow, Russia. At the time, it was still part of the Union of Soviet Socialist Republic. I happened to stumble across an immigrant as I was walking. I had a little chat with him and he told me how he ended up in Russia. He said he had was able to sneak successfully onto a ship, and able to make it into Russia safely. He had since straightened out his paperwork and was working on finishing his education. I asked him how he planned to overcome the language barrier. He replied that he was learning the language from scratch and was willing to do whatever it took, to integrate with his new found homeland. I walked away from that conversation inspired by this young man's positive outlook and drive to make something of himself.

When dating older women, if you have aspirations, you will have the same effect on them as the immigrant had on me. Your drive and outlook will energize them and remind them of how they once were at your age. That energy you generate will cause you to become desirable to them, because you've awakened their inner child. Youth is something most people try to hold on to. Older women are aware of their reality and embrace it. Never ask an older woman her age. She will tell it to you at her own choosing. Once she reveals her age, don't act surprised at the age gap. It might even be a generational gap. You have to be genuinely interested in getting to know an older woman if you want her to respond positively to you. They can see through false pretense because they've been around for a while, and have encountered all kinds of scenarios. There is nothing you can slip by them. King Solomon, the wisest man who has ever lived, and the world's greatest lover said, "It does no good to spread a net when the bird you are trying to catch is watching." A lot of younger men might show interest in an older woman just to see what it's like to date one. Don't expect to get too far if you think you can rush her into something she's not ready for.

The way you approach an older woman is by using the direct approach. Introduce yourself, and have a regular conversation. Once again, don't try to use lines or gimmicks in an effort to impress her. She's seen it all. If you make a good first impression and can carry a conversation that has substance, you won't have problems building a relationship with her. All older women love to dance. They will rarely turn you down if you invite them to go out dancing, when they are free. As a matter of fact, once they get to know you, they'll be the ones asking you to go dancing with them.

Some of the hurdles you'll face when dating older women are: They oftentimes make age an issue. Every now and then you'll have to re-affirm them that you're not bothered by the age gap. That's all they are looking for from you. Also sometimes they will unknowingly try to mold you into the person they want you to be, rather than adapt to the relationship. Something else you shouldn't ignore is that they tend to have emotional wounds from their previous relationships, if they never sought help to heal those wounds. So if you ever make such a woman angry and she's the yelling type, she may not really be yelling at you, she may actually be yelling at her ex-whatever. That's what's referred to as redirected anger. That's the reason I emphasize that you have to make sure that the women you are involved with are emotionally sound.

The good thing about them is once they get past the age issue, get rid of the baggage and are whole, they will open up your mind to their beautiful world, filled with delightful experiences and adventures. If you are thinking of dating one, be sure to add an album of ABBA to your music collection. It will evoke nostalgia in her.

Quality Relationships

Overall, you have to seek quality relationships in all areas of your life. Surround yourself with people who recognize your value. I have described the different cultural and ethnic backgrounds of women you will encounter as you seek the person with whom you feel the most compatible. It's up to you to choose what kind of woman best suits you. Use the information in this book to help you exercise sound judgment when choosing a mate. The purest form of love is when both people are willing to unselfishly give to each other with no strings attached. You have to believe in love in order to experience it in its fullness. If you are cynical because of some past disappointments you have faced, it will be very hard for you to discern true love even when it's in your midst.

The degree of reciprocity between the two of you will grow as the relationship grows. When you meet the person you are compatible with, the more the relationship grows, the less emotional strife you should experience. Arguments should get fewer as time goes by.

You should leave the days of toxic relationships behind you. Make up your mind that you will never settle for less than what you truly deserve, and you will draw quality people into your life. Screen those you let get close to you for loyalty. That should be the standard you measure the quality of all your relationships. I talk about loyalty because as you improve your life, people will notice the changes in you. There are some who will befriend you with good intentions, and then there are others who will do so, with their own selfish interests at heart. You have to become a student of human behavior, not just by reading this book, but also by going to the battlefield on the frontlines, and applying this knowledge. When I say battlefield I am talking about the real world where all the action is.

Become observant and pay attention to what people say when you first meet them. Have you noticed that the people who write "Tell All" books or those who try to screw others out of business deals and in their personal lives, have one thing in common? They are usually people who were able to weave their way into someone else's life, normally of higher status, and once the person of higher status fully trusted them, they were betrayed. If you're a man of quality, the way to overcome betrayal is by making sure that the people you have chosen to trust have something to lose too. If you allow people who have nothing to lose to have unlimited access to you, why should they be loyal to you?

In life, your greatest setbacks and disappointments, whether it is in relationships, spiritual life, business dealings, or even on your job, are likely to be caused by your very own kind. They are the ones who are most likely to hinder you from moving forward, and will try to hold you back if an opportunity arises for you to advance in life. Just because they are a bird of a feather doesn't necessarily mean you can count on them.

However, the people who are likely to be loyal and reach out to you in helping you succeed in achieving your dreams and goals, are most likely to be those who are culturally or even racially different than you. The story of "The Good Samaritan" wasn't recorded in scripture by accident. So you have to be cautious not be to too quick to judge those who are culturally or racially different than you based on what you do not know about them. They may turn out to be your greatest allies.

Chapter 12

Seven Maintenance Tips

Failure to admit you have a problem will not make it go away, it simply means you are in denial about your reality.

- *e*Nigma

1. The first step to solving a problem is to acknowledge that one exists. Even alcoholics understand this principle. Every relationship will be tested by life itself to see if it will stand the test of time. The key to preventing an avalanche of problems from happening is by constantly being able to feel the pulse of the relationship.

In Texas, the cops have what we call speed traps. A speed trap is normally set up in an area where cops anticipate drivers will be speeding. Another purpose is to nab drivers who are under the influence of alcohol, because in the south, we have enough drunk drivers. After they set up a speed trap, they'll go on a stake out, waiting for unsuspecting drivers to fall into their trap. At the turn of the century, or should I say millennium, I was driving about 15 miles over the speed limit and fell into one of these traps. Now I don't drink or smoke, I just happened to have a heavy foot on this particular day. The cop pulled me over and said, "I can see you're driving a little too fast, are you in a hurry to get somewhere?" To which I replied, "Yes, I am expecting a very important phone call from my mother, she's supposed to be calling me on my landline, and I don't want to miss her call." The cop didn't hesitate to write me a ticket because it was obvious to him that I was trying to be a wise-guy. I later on worked on a project with an off duty cop who told me, if you ever get stopped for speeding, don't try to talk your way out of a ticket; simply admit that you were speeding.

A few years later, I was speeding, and once again a cop came after me. I didn't see him immediately so I continued driving. He became furious and turned on his lights and hooted his horn. The problem was that there was no shoulder for me to pull over. Eventually I went over the curb and stopped. My guest who was sitting in the passenger seat of my vehicle said, "The cop must really be upset because you didn't stop immediately." I shrugged my shoulders and waited for him to approach. The cop then asked me, "Didn't you see me driving by your side when I was trying to slow you down?" I answered, "I didn't see you or else I would have slowed down." He asked me for my driver's license then went into his vehicle, and stayed there for about seven minutes. My guest said that usually when cops spend a considerable amount of time in their vehicles, they are writing you up on several violations. The cop finally emerged from his vehicle, handed me back my license and said, "I'll let you slide this time, but you have to drive the same speed as everybody else." I shook his hand and thanked him, then drove off.

I had learned several years before that you're a lot better off admitting you committed a traffic violation, rather than trying to be evasive about your faults. The cop sensed I was sincere, and by me saying, "I didn't see you, or else I would have slowed down," I was acknowledging that I was at fault. I have since been stopped for speeding three more times, and on all three occasions, the cops let me slide because I quickly acknowledged my fault.

In 2008, we witnessed the failure of mortgage giants Fannie Mae and Freddie Mac, because they refused to acknowledge their problems. They had implemented a practice of extending loans to those who couldn't afford them, and when the borrowers stopped paying their monthly notes, these mortgage companies were stuck with bad loans. It had a ripple effect that affected several financial institutes like: Lehman Brothers, Bear Stearns, Merrill Lynch, Washington Mutual, Wachovia, AIG, and many more. All this could have been avoided if they had tackled the issue earlier on, before it became a problem. That's why it is very important for you to calibrate and feel the pulse of your relationship to make sure you and your mate are on the same page.

In your relationships, you have to apply the principle of admitting or acknowledging your mistakes when you make them. That's a sign of both humility and maturity. Failure to admit you have a problem will not make it go away, it simply means you are in denial about your reality. Each party has to acknowledge their role in creating the problem, before it can be resolved.

2. Be willing to listen to others who might be able to help you solve your problem. However, you should also use your gut feeling and sound judgment in determining how you'll tackle the problem, or prevent one from happening.

On the week of Palm Sunday in April 2006, I happened to be in Vatican City. Some friends of mine were staying at the Grand Hotel Ritz in Rome, and wanted me to show them around the city, since I am familiar with it. I called Rino, a friend of mine who had a mini van, and asked him to give me a ride to meet my other friends. The hotel was on busy street called Via Chelini. As I was getting out of the mini van, somehow my wallet slipped out of my pocket and dropped right in the middle of the street. The wallet had almost one thousand Euros in it, my debit cards, driver's license, and my social security card. I didn't notice anything unusual, because the street was so busy; I just was trying to navigate through the traffic.

Rino drove ahead, to look for a parking spot, while I headed for the hotel. His wife stayed in the van and waited for us. After we arrived, we asked the receptionist to page the other friends of mine who were expecting me. They apparently had stepped out, so we decided to wait for a few minutes. After a while, I suggested to Rino that we leave, and I'd come back another day to see them. All this time, I wasn't aware that I had lost my wallet. We got into the van and Rino started to drive off. We were about five minutes away from the hotel, when Rino made a U-turn and insisted that I at least leave a note to indicate to my friends that I had dropped by. I resisted but he insisted that it was the Italian way of showing courtesy. I figured, when in Rome do as the Romans, so I agreed to go back to the hotel on Via Chelini.

No sooner had we entered the lobby than the receptionist ran toward us and said, "I believe one of you dropped your wallet; here it is." Rino looked at me and said, "That's yours." I felt my pockets and indeed I was missing my wallet. I asked the receptionist, "Where did you find it?" The receptionist answered, "A stranger who refused to identify himself said he found it in the middle of the street, and knew from its size that the person who owned it must be in the Grand Hotel Ritz." I looked into the wallet and everything was intact. Nothing was missing. I thanked the receptionist for being honest, and wanted to offer a financial gift for the honesty, but the receptionist would not take any money from me. I proceeded to write a note and left it for my friends, and then Rino and I left.

I was very thankful that I listened to Rino's advice when he insisted that we go back to the hotel. His gut feeling was able to sense that which I was unable to sense. He sensed that it would be beneficial to me to return to the hotel, and indeed he was right. I always surround myself with people who have discernment because they can correct my focus when I am off track.

There are times when a trusted outside ally might be able to help you rectify what is plaguing your relationship. Someone on the outside might be able to see that which you are oblivious to. They themselves might have encountered your situation before, so that qualifies them to offer you advice. Don't be too close-minded and shut out those who are trying to reach out to you with good intentions. I also mentioned that not only should you be willing to seek advice from others, but you should also use your gut feeling and sound judgment in determining how you yourself will tackle the problem, or prevent one from happening.

That same week when I lost and found my wallet, I decided to go to Piazza Venezia late Saturday afternoon, on the day before Palm Sunday. Piazza Venezia is a very popular open public square in Rome. As I was walking down a particular street that leads to the Piazza, I had a gut feeling that I should cross immediately and walk on the other side of the street. I was compliant, and to my astonishment, as soon as I crossed to the other side, over 10,000 pounds of heavy metal scaffolding collapsed on the exact side of the street I was walking. I could have been squashed and buried beneath the heavy metal if I hadn't listened to that inner voice. I was so shaken I cancelled all my plans to go to Piazza Venezia and just went back to my hotel room. I can only conclude that it was the unseen hand of God that not only rescued my wallet, but also saved my life that week.

In any relationship, you too should use your gut feeling and sound judgment to help you prevent a problem from occurring. For instance, if you're in a relationship and notice that the other person feels uncomfortable talking about certain subjects, don't press them to participate in conversations regarding that which you know causes them discomfort. Also do not reopen old wounds out of anger, or reveal any confidentiality that they have trusted you with. It doesn't help the relationship grow. It is better for you to prevent problems from happening rather than try to fix them. Your goal is to maintain a healthy relationship not create a toxic one.

3. There will always be an opposing voice from a third party that will try to influence your relationship in a negative way. Don't grant them access to your loved ones.

Not everybody is looking out for you. Believe me, there are those who always strike out in relationships and hope your relationship fails too. It makes them feel better about themselves that they are not alone in their misery. They will oppose the choice of woman you court, without any justification. Their intention is to break you up.

One summer in 1999, I was in Dallas Texas driving to a meeting. One thing that struck me the most was that the cars seemed to be stalling for almost half a mile. It was early in the morning and the freeway shouldn't have had a traffic jam. I couldn't imagine why the traffic was slow. I patiently waited to get to my exit. As I approached the exit, I noticed something else unusual. There were cars parked on the side, right below the overpass, and the motorists we standing outside yelling something. I found the whole spectacle to be intriguing so I decided to investigate and see what all the commotion was about.

Several hundred feet above the freeway, was a man standing at the edge of the overpass attempting to grow wings. He had given up on life and wanted to take his own life by leaping into the busy traffic below him. The man had one of his legs over the concrete blocks and it seemed that he'd soon be joining his ancestors. Behind him was an entire squad of police officers yelling at him, "Don't jump! Don't jump!" Below him, the motorists were yelling, "Jump! Jump!" I had never witnessed anything like this before in my life.

There will come a point in your relationship when you might feel like giving up on it due to unavoidable circumstances. The discouragement could be caused by loss of your job, demotion, loss of a loved one, or unfounded rumors. That's when you'll be very susceptible to listening to the third party who might tell you to let go of the relationship because it is not worth the effort. They might even intentionally discourage you to abandon your relationship because they want to replace you. People who want to sincerely help you will encourage you to stay the course and work things out if the relationship is a healthy one.

Luckily, the man in Dallas who was trying to take his life, was successfully tackled by the cops, and what initially appeared would result in a tragic ending, had a happy ending.

The same will happen to you if you ignore the voices that are trying to speak death into your relationship. Your ability to discern what's authentic from what's fake will save you a lot of headaches. You should aim at accentuating the positive in your relationship, because what you feed your relationship is what it will reproduce. If you feed it with voices of doubt and uncertainty, you might end up talking yourself out of a promising relationship. Don't base the quality and longevity of your relationships on the opinions of the mediocre bystanders, the naysayers, or the button-pushers. They will use every opportunity they have to destroy, rather than breathe life into your meaningful relationships.

4. Keep The Lines Of Communication Open. The effectiveness with which you resolve conflict will depend on how well you communicate in your relationship. It is very important that you are on the same page at all times with your mate. This eliminates any misunderstanding and helps maintain the equilibrium of the emotional and mental bond that holds the relationship together, even during your absence.

You have to nurture the most important relationships in your life no matter how well you feel things are going. I personally travel a lot to distant lands. During my travels, I make it a point to take some time out, to write a brief letter, or send a post card to those who are close to me. I am one of the very few people who still write handwritten notes. People are always appreciative when they receive handwritten letters or notes. It is quite different from an e-mail, which can be deleted instantly with a punch of a button.

On October 25, 1998, I received a letter from my best friend who had been deployed and was traveling on the USS Dwight Eisenhower, which is a navy ship. As I was crisscrossing America on road trips, my best friend was sailing the seas around the world on a boat. We always made it a point to keep in touch with each other no matter how far we were apart. The same applied to my parents, siblings and friends. Because I want to teach by example, I have included for you a few of the numerous letters from my collection in the next chapter. They are responses to communication I sent to the recipients during my travels.

Nonverbal communication is not the only way to communicate effectively. Verbal communication is just as effective. Whenever there is a misunderstanding, I recommend you communicate your feelings in person, and not by phone, e-mail, text-message, or snail mail. In person, the other party is able to tell if you are sincere or not.

5. Patience will take you a long way. Practice it. People will disappoint you. They will fail you. Nobody is flawless. We all have our shortcomings. Patience is the one characteristic you'll have to implement even when you don't feel like doing so. Some quality women may be slow learners, they may not have domestic skills or they simply may not have etiquette. You might have a quality woman who is untidy. Perhaps when you look into her car, she has clothes, roller blades, books, and all kinds of items all over the place. Maybe the inside of her garage is at sixes and sevens, that's why she parks outside. All this does not make her a bad woman. She is still worthy of your heart. She simply needs order in her life. As a man of quality, take the lead and point her to the right direction. Your patience while helping your woman overcome these impediments will be extremely necessary, in order to avoid being frustrated with the whole relationship.

When a friend of mine first met his wife, she knew nothing about cooking. Her mother hadn't taught her the necessary domestic skills required to sustain a home. She only knew how to thaw. After they were married, he taught her how to cook from scratch. My friend knew it would be expensive to eat out in restaurants all the time so he did something about it. He sent her to "Cook School" where she took additional cooking lessons. She turned out to be an excellent cook. The meals she prepares rival any restaurant dish I have ever been served. After you eat one of her meals, you can't help but say, "Bravissima!" Even though she was a quality woman, she was deficient in that area. Her husband's patience and understanding turned her into a well-balanced wife. They have been married for over 25 years.

On June 15, 2007, I was at Fiumicino airport in Rome waiting at the baggage claim conveyor. I had been invited to attend a series of concerts in Bologna Italy, by some friends, but I wanted to first make a stop in Rome. When I flew in from Gatwick airport in London, my luggage somehow pulled a disappearing act, so I arrived in Rome empty handed. I filed a lost baggage claim, and left my contact information at the terminal after about three hours of waiting at the baggage claim area.

I thought I was just having a bad day, but things even got worse. I went to my hotel room and was slowly unwinding when I received a phone-call that there was a high likelihood that my lost luggage had been recovered. I called a friend who was kind enough to give me a ride to the airport. We were about five blocks from my hotel on our way to the airport, when a gypsy driving a scooter ran a red light and bumped into us in the middle of the intersection. He and his scooter ended up on top of the hood of my friend's car, and the car's windshield got completely smashed by the impact. Luckily we were wearing shades and none of the glass from the shattered windshield caused any physical damage to us.

First it was the lost baggage, now this. We called the cops, but in Italy it takes forever for them to arrive. The gypsy had no insurance, but the good thing is that no one was hurt. We had to wait for almost two more hours before a female officer showed up late that evening. After we filed a report, I was able to get another ride, and eventually retrieved my baggage from the airport. I went back to my hotel, and reflected on these experiences, which were real life lessons for me to exercise patience even when everything seemed to be going wrong. You too will encounter unexpected setbacks in life. Patience is something that doesn't get better with time. Marketers understand this very well, and do nothing to encourage you to be patient. We live in a society that wants to see instant results. In the food industry, they have pills that promise people they can lose weight in just a matter of weeks, or gain muscle in a short amount of time. They take advantage of society's impatience. You also have fast food restaurants, and microwave dinners, both of which serve the same purpose of instant fulfillment.

The financial sector is no different. Because they understand that society is filled with impatient people, they have devised a solution to feed your impatience. They came up with Payday Advance centers for those who don't have the patience to wait for their paychecks from the company they work for. How were our parents able to make it without all these conveniences we have today? They were able to do so because they understood the importance and value of patience. Patience forges character.

If you bring the mindset of impatience into your personal relationships, you'll be more concerned about seeing instant results than allowing the relationship to grow at its own natural pace. I've known people who started off on the right foot, but because they rushed to move in together, the relationship fell apart within months. There were others who were quick to apply for lines of credit in both people's names, only to find out that the other person wasn't financially responsible. A practitioner of the natural approach should not have to be hurried into anything or hurry someone else into something that's against the other person's conscious. Patience is a useful tool in helping you empathize with other people, and can also help you build restraint. Your patience training will happen in real life scenarios, and the result of that boot camp will yield a disciplined life and a fulfilling relationship.

6. Learn To Forgive. At some point the woman you are dating will do or say something offensive. What are you going to do about it? Perhaps you might discover that she still has pictures of an ex-boyfriend, or listened to unfounded rumors about you and believed them. She might make an offensive comment about one of your family members or ridicule your friends. Offense comes in different forms. If she's been a great and loyal woman and is compatible with you, you'll have to forgive her and let bygones be bygones. Unforgiveness breeds resentment, which eventually manifests itself through bitterness. Some of the most unforgiving people are the saddest people you'll ever meet. It can even affect one's health. I believe there are people who have health problems not because of an unhealthy diet or not exercising, but because they are plagued with unforgiveness.

If you were once in an unhealthy relationship with a woman, forgiving her doesn't mean you should take her back. However, you can't let her past actions prevent you from building new and healthy relationships with other women. When you forgive her, you are relieving yourself of the burden and cloud of bitterness. Nobody wants to be around someone bitter. Forgiveness does not mean you approve the other person's behavior, nor does it mean you are weak. It means you have mastered the art of letting go of an offense. It is not contingent upon an apology. Chances are, the offender might not even be aware that what they are doing is offensive.

I was once dating a woman who liked to wear super-realistic weaves. It was during the Super Bowl half time that we both started to horseplay. She was trying to wrestle with me, and during that time, I accidentally pulled her weave off her head. I never knew that beneath the weave, she wore a funny stocking on her head to cover her natural hair. I chuckled because I had never seen her without a weave. She was so offended, she snatched the weave from my hand, and was almost in tears. I apologized to her instantly, and because she had a forgiving spirit, she didn't hold it against me. She knew that I did not pull the wig off with the intention of embarrassing her. That is an illustration of doing something offensive to someone, and not being aware that your actions offended the person. She was mature enough to realize that for any relationship to survive, it's imperative to extend forgiveness to the offender.

I mentioned earlier that on June 15, 2007, I was in Rome on my way to Bologna to enjoy the festivities, when I lost my luggage at the airport. After I recovered my luggage, I bought a train ticket and headed north to Bologna, early the next morning. The fastest way to travel in Europe is to use the EuroStar train system. When I arrived in Bologna, someone was already waiting for me at the train station. After touring the city, I got some rest in preparation for the concert that was happening the following day.

We arrived at the venue on time and after everybody was seated, the two performers requested everyone to turn off their cell phones. One of the performers played the piano, while the other played the violin. I believe the concert was also being recorded live for release on video. About four minutes into the concert, a woman's cell phone rang. She was sitting in the second row and almost everyone seemed visibly upset with her for the rude interruption.

Something interesting happened thereafter. Knowing that the audience was upset, the pianist quickly improvised by duplicating the ring tone of the cell phone. He repeated the melody, and the violinist too improvised. Because the concert was being recorded, rather than chastising the lady, they helped her save face. The musicians created a completely improvised tune by duplicating the ring tone of her cell phone for the next five minutes. It was comical, but also showed the genius of the performers, who were able to play by ear.

At the end of the improvised tune, the audience that was originally agitated by the woman's actions stood up and applauded the performance, and was very forgiving toward her. The performers then resumed playing the original tune they were playing before the cell phone interruption.

The lesson I learned that evening was that sometimes in life, you shouldn't take yourself too seriously. Learn to have fun even when you make mistakes. When you do make a mistake, don't be too hard on yourself. Cut yourself some slack. It's not the end of the world. You should have that same attitude when it comes to your personal relationships.

7. Preparation Will Be Your Most Important Key To Enjoying Successful And Fulfilling Relationships. Lack of preparation has cost people countless relationships. When you fail to prepare, you run out of options. Teachers understand the importance of preparation, that's why they give their students homework and quizzes, to prepare them for the final exams. In order to have a healthy relationship, you have to prepare yourself for the kind of person you desire, just as you would prepare yourself for a job interview, or a speech. I hear many people describe the kind of person they want, but are doing nothing in their lives to prepare themselves for that kind of person. When the person happens to arrive, the relationship doesn't last long because one person was ill prepared for the other. If you refuse to prepare, you will not know how to handle the unexpected. How do you prepare? Well, I have solved that problem for you by writing this book. Reading this book will prepare you for the different scenarios life will throw at you. You will know what to expect when handling the different types of women I have described in my book. You also have this maintenance chapter to guide you.

I only give sound advice. It has been battle-tested and has all checked out. I have to remind you again that I myself am not a doctor, or psychiatrist. I am a scientist who specializes in the study of human behavior. The knowledge, wisdom, and insight I possess, was acquired on the frontlines and in the trenches, right on the battlefield of life. Nothing in this book can be refuted by any expert or medical practitioner in the field of psychiatry, psychology, or psychotherapy. I am willing to debate any one of them anytime, regarding the accuracy of my findings.

Of all the three ingredients I've mentioned, insight is perhaps the most important one. It is strongly reinforced by the scientists Hergenhahn and Olson who summarize the principle of insightful learning, based on Gestaltists as follows:

Insightful learning is usually regarded as having four characteristics:

1. *The transition from presolution to solution is sudden and complete.*

2. *Performance based on a solution gained by insight is usually smooth and free of errors.*

3. *A solution to a problem gained by insight is retained for a considerable length of time.*

4. *A principle gained by insight is easily applied to other problems.*

You are now armed and dangerous with my principles, and your new inner man. Do the things I have listed in this book, and you will thank me.

In the south, they take barbeques very seriously. If you're invited to one, you better show up or else you'll have a lot of explaining to do. In June 1998, I was on a road trip driving through Oklahoma. Sure enough, I got a phone call from friends who invited me to a barbeque. The barbeque was going to take place at the Red Rock Canyon, which is a state park. There was a winding road that is several feet deep that lead to the bottom of the canyon. I had never been to the place so we met at a certain location, and I followed my friends down to the bottom of the canyon.

Knowing that Oklahoma is in tornado alley, we left the car radio on the weather station as we enjoyed the barbeque. We were playing a game called 'Horse Shoes' when a weather alert was issued over the radio. A tornado had touched down, and was bringing with it heavy rains. Upon listening further, we learned that the tornado was headed our way. We quickly packed the barbeque grills and drove behind a convoy of vehicles that was already ahead of us. We all made it to the top without incident and drove west to seek shelter.

As we were driving, I noticed about half a dozen cars from a distance driving east to our direction. I thought the people were crazy because the weather channel was advising motorists to go west, or seek nearby shelter. I recognized weather radar dishes mounted on their vehicles. These people were storm chasers. I had only seen them on television on the Discovery Channel and National Geographic, now I had a chance to get a close look at them and the equipment they use. The storm chasers weren't fazed by the seriousness of the storm. They just wanted to find its exact location. My friends and I finally found a safe place to take shelter and all we had to do was wait. The storm chasers were now out of view. The winds were very strong as the rains pounded on the roof of the building in which we had sought refuge. After about two hours, it subsided, and it was now safe for us to continue on to our destination. Perhaps the storm chasers were successful in finding the location of the storm. That is something I'll never know. Nevertheless, based on the information released on the weather station, there were no casualties from the storm, which means the storm chasers were unharmed.

Every relationship will have its storms, so you have to prepare yourself to deal with any crisis that comes along. Each woman has a different temperament, which means you will have to adapt, in order to successfully diffuse a crisis at hand.

Sometimes you have to confront storms in order to experience redemption. The redemptive value storm chasers get from confronting storms is that they are able to collect data that enables them to accurately predict any future storms. The result of being able to accurately predict future storms is that human lives are kept out of harm's way because it gives people enough time to prepare for any contingencies.

The redemptive value you will get from confronting storms in your relationship is that you will learn more about yourself and about the person with whom you are involved. When you are well prepared to handle conflict, you might even end up salvaging a relationship that was in emotional dire straits.

Have you ever wondered why the wise man built his house upon the rock? It's because, just like the storm chasers, he too believed in confronting his storms; and when the rain came tumbling down …you know the rest of the story.

It is imperative that you study and absorb my principles to increase your odds in the dating arena. Later on in life, you can then pass on this information to your sons and nephews. I know the immediate question that comes to mind is, "What if all men study your principles, won't there be too much competition? Won't some other guy with this material try to out-alpha me?" Relax. You don't have to worry about that. Women will always outnumber men. Mother nature is on your side. This will also force women to evolve qualitatively, in order to attract quality men. So it's a win-win situation.

Chapter 13

Travel Log

This is the building I mention in chapter twelve where the actual scaffolding collapsed about five seconds after I crossed the street. I was able to walk away unharmed and lived to tell my story. Taken by me in real time in April 2006 in Rome, Italy.

This building was about five blocks ahead of me. It is a different building but gives you an idea of what scaffolding is like. Imagine the weight of all this collapsing on your head. This photo was taken the same day as the previous one.

These are tickets for the metro in Rome. It is best to buy the ones on the left for four Euros because they are good for 24 hours as opposed to the ones on the right that are only good for 75 minutes and cost one Euro.

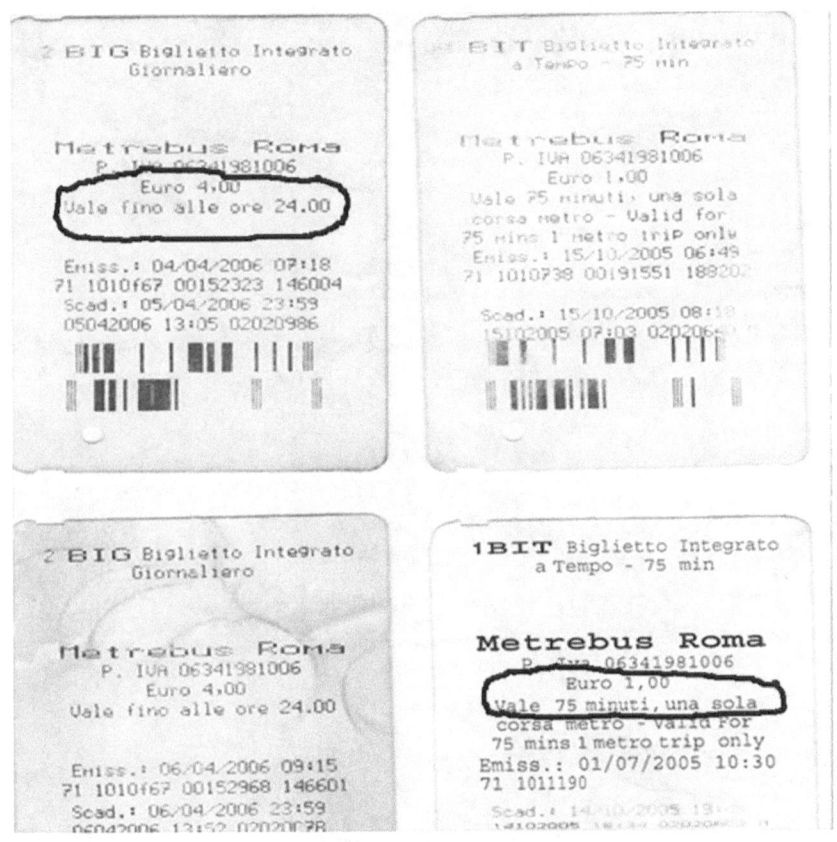

Underground train (tube) ticket to visit my cousin in Stratford, England, mentioned in chapter three.

One of my airline tickets to Rome.

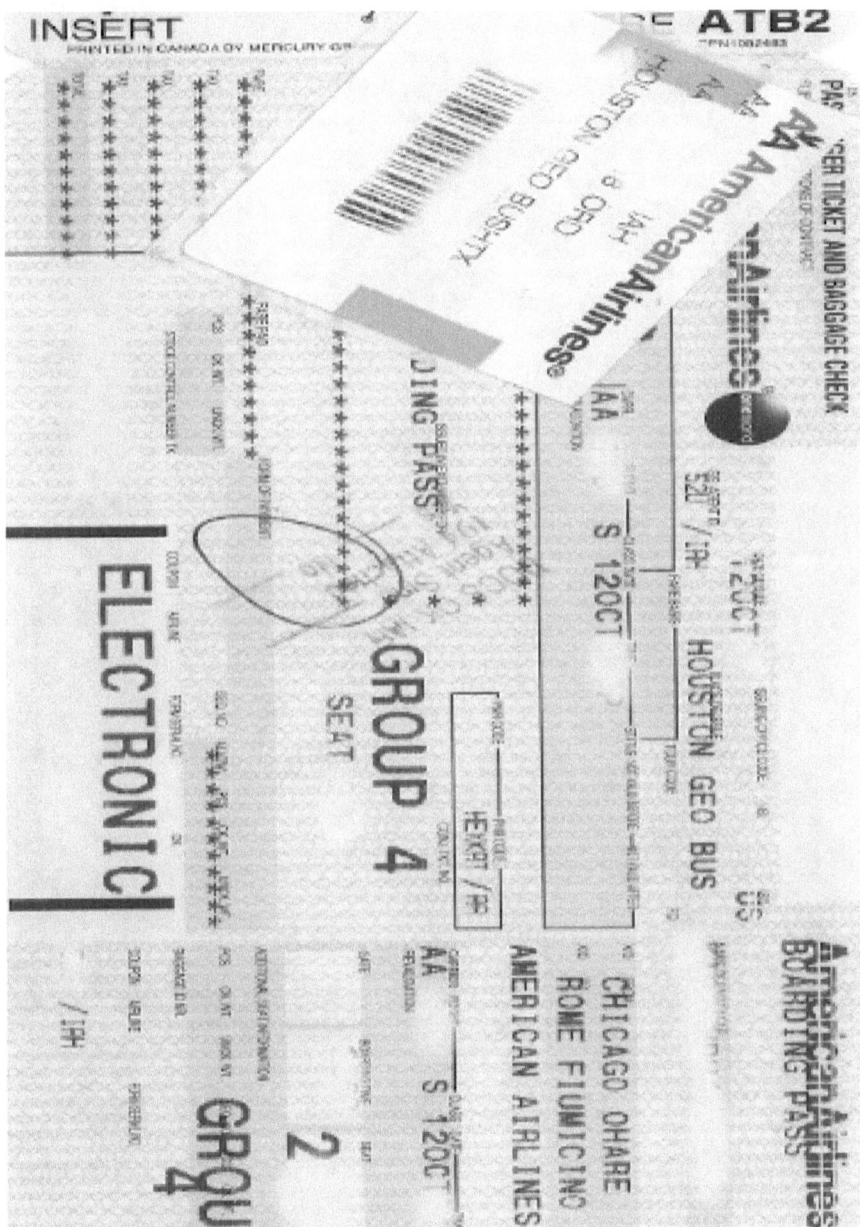

An airline ticket from London to Houston in 2007.

This is the trip mentioned in chapter twelve, where my baggage was lost and then found. I had to file this baggage claim. It is the same trip where we got bumped by a gypsy.

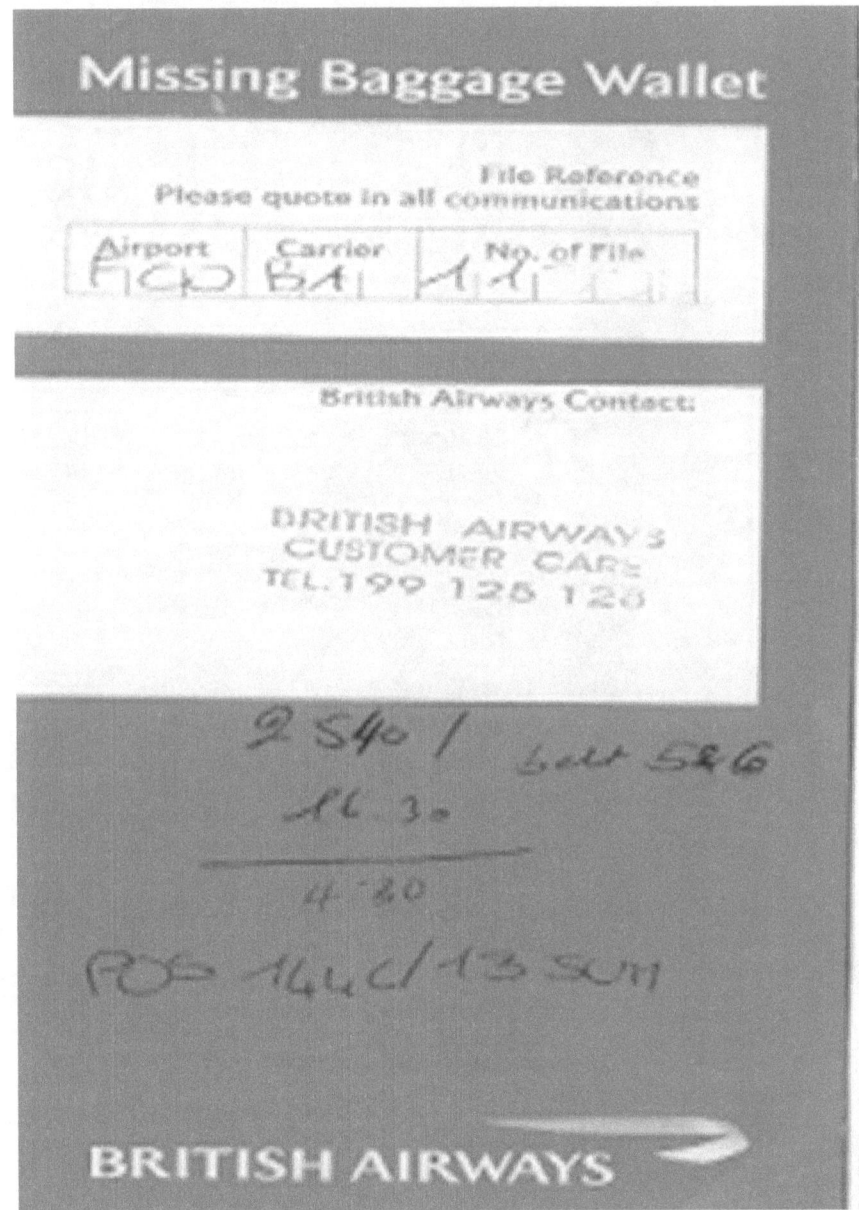

The ticket for my adventurous trip to Moscow in August 1992 that I mentioned. Russia was still part of the Soviet Socialist Republic.

During my travels, I always make it a point to have fun. Theater is my cup of tea, especially if I'm with a hottie.

This is a receipt for a train ticket to Bologna, Italy from Rome. This is the trip where I was invited to music festivities in chapter twelve.

The train ticket on the top is from Venice (Venezia) to Rome, and the one below is a ticket from Florence (Firenze) to Rome. It is the trip in 2005 that I talked about where a young couple kept kicking my feet, to prevent me from falling asleep.

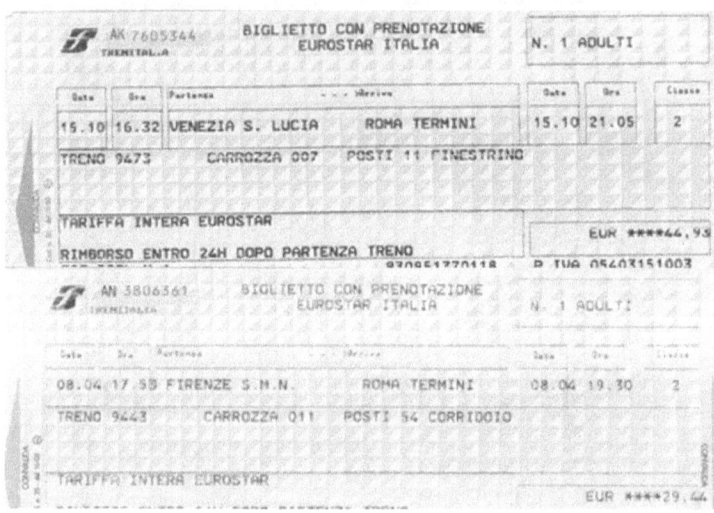

In Europe, the easiest way to handle meals is by snacking. A typical snack costs about five Euros.

When I accidentally dropped my wallet in the middle of a busy street in Rome, this is the hotel I had visited, where an identified stranger left it. See chapter twelve.

This is what a ticket to the Vatican museums looks like. They observe a very strict dress code. Women cannot wear short-sleeved dresses or blouses and cannot wear shorts to the Vatican. The Sistine chapel is in the Vatican museums.

Even on my trips, I still take some time out to send my friends postcards. For demonstration purposes, I have included in this section just a few pieces of communication to show how I interact with my friends and family, and their responses.

As I was crisscrossing America on road trips in 1998, my best friend was sailing the seas on the USS Dwight D. Eisenhower.

This is a postcard from a very lovely friend of mine.

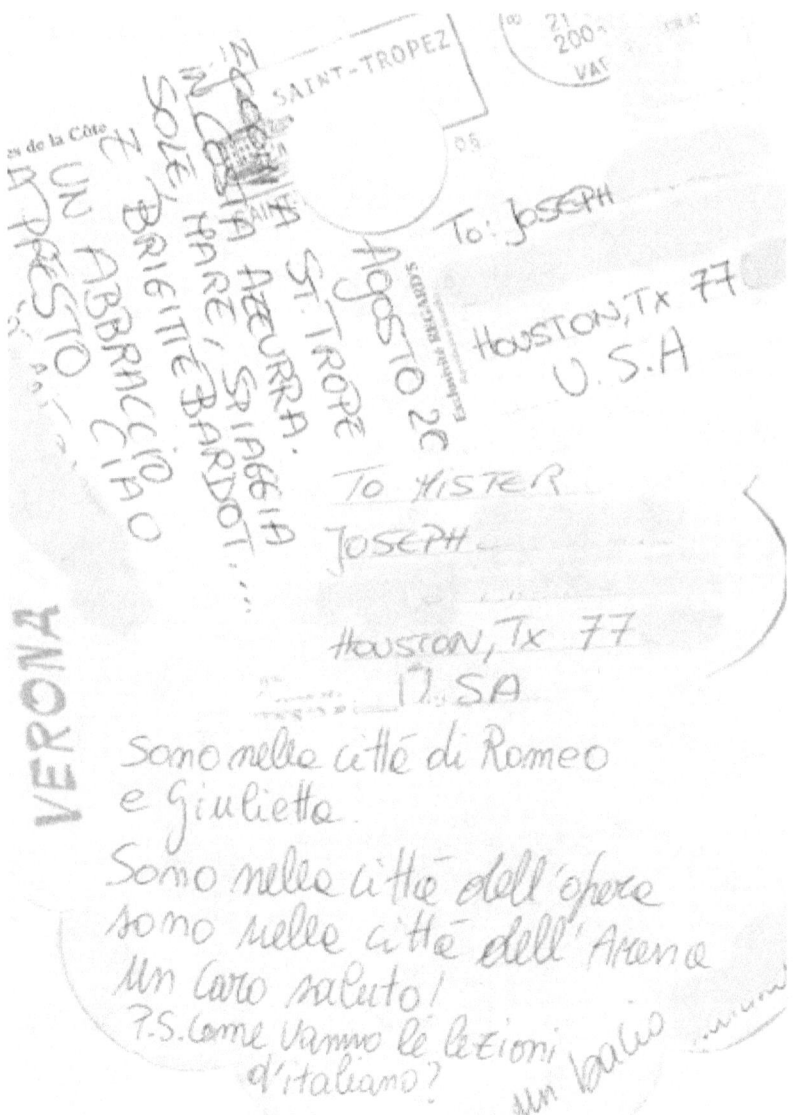

My friends and family know that I prefer receiving letters to e-mails, so they send me handwritten ones. This is a letter from my brother.

A letter from my sister. She's the one I talked about in chapter nine who made me breakfast, and because I only ate the scrambled eggs and not the tomatoes, she hasn't cooked for me again. But I'm cool like that.

Dear Joseph
How are you? Thanks so
much for my CD and Tape
I love Bebe so much and
Cece as well. How are you
doing. Thanks for your
advice regarding the
readings. I love
aust in Pr
me as
my
a
in
to
up
for
hope
tried
Joseph

Please use
the Postcode

Joseph

HOUSTON
TEXAS
77

all exc

A letter from another one of my sisters. I mention her in chapter two.

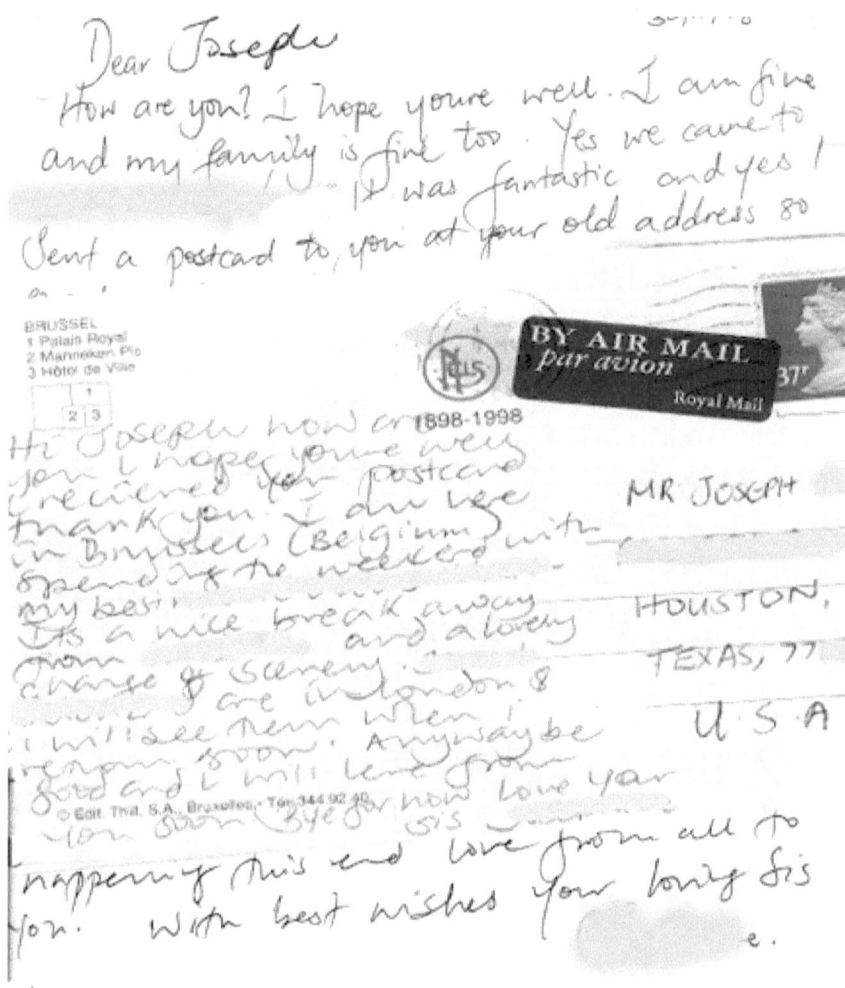

A letter from her majesty - my Mom

My dearest Joseph
I hope you are O.K. & that
everything goes on well with
you.
This is just to thank you for
my Mother's Day card and
the ▓▓▓ May thanks
for everything.
We are all keeping well here
although ▓▓▓ with
sometimes.
▓▓▓ is giving Birth
to her Baby Boy in July 11th 2008
O.K dear, I must go now
Bye for now
your loving mother
Mrs ▓▓▓

A letter from the big boss – my Dad

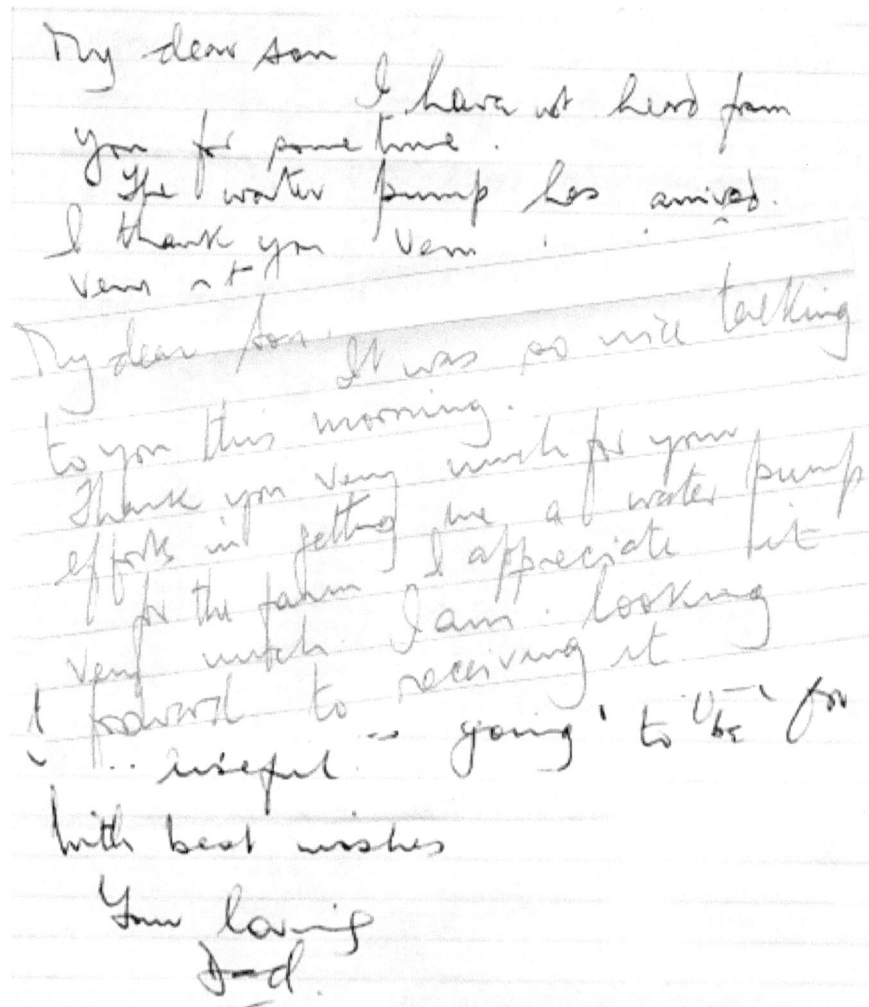

I drew this picture with my very own hand in January 1997 using black-ink pen. Little did I know that over a decade later, it would make the front cover of my book. I continue to sketch and have accumulated a number of drawings.

Glossary

Alpha females tend to focus more on building relationships that revolve around their careers. They are ambitious and high achievers, and tend to define themselves by what they do for a living.

Alpha males are well-balanced men who exude confidence and a strong sense of self. They are not bothered by speculation or doubt, and tend to accomplish what they set their minds to. Alpha males are the most desirable to females because they're manly men.

Beta females on the other hand, are ambitious and high achievers too, but place greater importance on building meaningful personal relationships rather than business contacts. Whether or not you have any business dealing with a beta female, she will value your individuality and humanity. Betas even feel comfortable wearing dresses and embrace their femininity with pride.

Beta males tend to be spoilers. They see in alpha males that which they do not have, but wish to have. Unlike nomads who are openly hostile, beta males try to give you the impression that they are friendly and trustworthy, and once they earn your trust, they'll violate it in a heartbeat. They will embrace you with one hand, and stab you in the back with the other.

Bravissimo: Excellent. (Derived from the word bravo.)

Discernment: Being able to grasp and comprehend what is obscure, and stresses accuracy as in reading character, motives or knowing true friends.

Eye-candy: Something pleasing to the eyes.

Empirical: That which can be experienced with the five senses.

ETC: eNigma Technique of Courtship. A courtship method that applies the natural approach as a means of courtship. Invented by eNigma a.k.a Joseph.

Friend-girl: A woman with whom you have a platonic relationship.

Frontlines: Where all the action is on the dating scene.

Gentilissimo: Very gentle.

Girlfriend: The opposite of friend-girl. Think of a girlfriend as an upgraded version of a friend-girl.

Insight: The power or act of seeing through a situation.

Intimidation is when a person in a position of power tries to control a person of less power, using fear tactics.
La dolce vita: The sweet life.

Mandingo: The man.

Manipulation is when the person in a position of less power, tries to control the person in a position of influence.

Metro sexual is simply a man who is apologetic about his manliness.

Nafka: A woman who is loose. A slut.

Networking is the process of building business related contacts, mostly for self-serving purposes.

Nomad: A nomad in the dating game is a male who once was alpha, but lost his glory.

Psychology: The science of human behavior as defined by Walter Pillsbury.

Richissima: A very rich woman.

Sensualissimo: Very sensual.

Spit game: To score verbal points with a woman using smooth talk.

Notes

Robert Sternberg. "A triangular theory of love." Psychological Review, 1986.

Robert Sternberg. The Triangle of Love: Intimacy, Passion, and Commitment. New York: Basic Books, 1988.

National Oceanic and Atmospheric Administration.Tropical Storm Frances, September 11, 1998.

National Hurricane Center. Hurricane Ike, September 13, 2008.

Kevin Leman Ph.D. 7 Things He'll Never Tell You: Tyndale House Publishers, 2007.

GQ Magazine. An Interview with American soldiers from the Pennsylvania National Guard, June 2005.

King Solomon's Reign and Wisdom. Pr.1: 17; Pr 19:6. [970 B.C – 930 B.C.]

Tom Mortensen – Pell Institute for the Study of Opportunity in Higher Education.

US Census Bureau: College enrollment statistics – Gender gap, [1967-2000]

Walter Pillsbury. Psychology [is defined as] the science of human behavior, 1911.

Oprah Winfrey – Show Theme:"70% Of Black Women Are Single." [04/06/2007.]

YouTube video of Oprah Show – http://www.youtube.com/ watch?v=HvQel-sIKwM.

Hergenhahn and Olson. An Introduction To A History of Psychology – Sixth Edition   [pg 473]: Wadsworth Cengage Learning, 2005.

Larry Ruddell Ph.D. Business Ethics – Faith That Works: Halcyon Press, Ltd., 2004.

David Sue/Derald Wing Sue/Stanley Sue. Understanding Abnormal Behavior – 8th Ed.

Houghton Mifflin Company, 2006.

Diane E. Papalia/Sally Wendkos Olds/Ruth Duskin Feldman. Human Development

10th Ed – Triangular Subtheory of Love [pg 521] McGraw Hill, 2007

www.ingramcontent.com/pod-product-compliance
Lightning Source LLC
Chambersburg PA
CBHW061258280526
45784CB00002B/803